# How to Hire

www.amplifypublishing.com

For more information, please contact:
Amplify Publishing, an imprint of Amplify Publishing Group
620 Herndon Parkway, Suite 320
Herndon, VA 20170
info@amplifypublishing.com

Library of Congress Control Number: 2021923806

CPSIA Code: PRV0323A

ISBN-13: 978-1-64543-324-8

Printed in the United States

To SPO,

For believing in a busboy

# HOW TO
# HIRE

The Essential Guide to Recruit & Retain the Right People

## CLINT SMITH

**Founder & CEO, CareerPlug**

an imprint of Mascot Books

# CONTENTS

# INTRODUCTION

## ANYTHING IS POSSIBLE WITH
## THE RIGHT PEOPLE

I n 2007, I started CareerPlug with a laptop and a few thousand dollars. Now, it's grown to dozens of employees and over 17,000 clients. We couldn't have gotten here without making the right hires along the way.

Hiring is hard. When you get it right, it can create opportunities that you never imagined. When you get it wrong, it can make your business—and you—feel completely worthless.

I know it because I have lived it. I went from working alone in my apartment to making my first hire, then from running a small team where I managed everyone to growing a leadership team where I turned over almost everything to people who could do it better than me. I have felt the highs of hiring an intern and developing him into an exceptional leader and the lows of hiring the wrong leader and watching it almost destroy our culture.

There's a mountain on the cover of this book to represent the adventure of growing a business. The journey upward is tough—

sometimes unbearable. But it's so rewarding to look back and see the progress you have made along the way.

That mountain got a lot steeper in 2020.

I originally wrote this book in 2019. As I prepared to publish the following spring, the pandemic shut everything down. As businesses reopened and struggled to hire people, it became clear that the lessons in this book were needed more than ever.

But I also realized that the book was missing a final section (and that our software product was missing a key component): *How to retain your team and help them reach their potential.* Hiring well is not enough, especially today. You have to help your people grow, or else you will lose them.

Your company will not reach its potential—you will not make it to the top of the mountain—until you help your team reach their potential.

I want to be your guide and make your journey to the top a little easier, at least when it comes to people. In addition to growing my own business, I have personally worked with hundreds of leaders to learn how they hire and grow their teams. I have seen what worked well, what didn't work so well, and what failed miserably. These experiences helped us create our software product to help businesses hire and develop the right people.

This book is designed as an actionable guide, with bite-sized sections that you can implement immediately. And I weaved in our own story to help you see how we got here—and to throw in a few laughs at our expense.

I want to see you make the best hires and grow beyond your wildest expectations. My company would not be where it is today—I would not be where I am today—without the benefit of mentors and insightful advice along the way. Now I am paying it forward.

Happy Hiring!

CULTURE

# KNOW WHO YOU ARE

## CULTURE IS NOT A SIGN
## HANGING ON THE WALL

Hiring starts with culture.

Culture, more than anything else, is what attracts people to a company. It is what keeps them there. It is also what makes them leave. Your culture is a magnet: you attract the people you deserve. You cannot expect to attract warm, welcoming people if you have an aggressive, calculating culture.

Your culture is what you value. No, not the values framed on the wall—what you *really* value. Culture is who you are every day when you come to work. It's what you do and say. And it's how you treat others—externally and (especially) internally. It is what you do when others are not looking. Culture is not what you say it is—it's what your team says it is.

It took me a long time to figure this out.

Culture starts with you.

Culture was pretty easy when I founded CareerPlug, just me in my apartment. I knew what I valued: hard work, creativity, and a laid-back attitude. My first job out of college was in investment banking. It checked the box for hard work (60–80 hours a week), but it definitely wasn't creative or laid back. I wanted to work hard and build something special . . . and I wanted to do it wearing sandals every day. I lived that culture day and night for the first year of CareerPlug.

Things got tougher when I started to hire a few people.

I nailed my first hire, Garrett, who grew to become our finance leader. But I made mistakes with the others. I didn't look hard enough for my values. Some employees had lots of complaints, but no ideas on how to improve things. Others were laid back, but they were also unmotivated. Our culture changed, and suddenly, I did not know who we were as a company. We started losing money. It wasn't a coincidence.

We hit rock bottom one day; I don't even remember what happened now, but I was done. Something had to change.

I called Garrett after work and asked if he wanted to grab a beer. We met at a place called the Deep Eddy Cabaret, a 1970s time capsule of a bar west of downtown Austin. It was a dark and stormy night, and Garrett knew exactly what I wanted to discuss: we had to hit the reset button and rebuild the company.

The next morning, my birthday, I fired our other two employees. I'll never forget that feeling. It wasn't completely sickening (there was definitely some relief), but I knew that I never wanted to feel like that again.

We were more careful when we made our next hire, David, who worked out great. A decade later, David was leading our product and marketing teams. But, looking back, I know I got lucky. I had still not been clear on what we needed in someone.

I only had a breakthrough once I wrote our mission, vision, and values with our team. We clarified our purpose and strengthened our commitment to it by writing it down. Everything—from the people we needed to surround ourselves with to the very product that we needed to produce—became clear after that. And that clarity has been critical to our growth and guided the decisions we made along the way. This includes the decision to become a remote company. Ultimately, we decided that we valued access to nationwide talent and increased flexibility over all of us being together at an office in Austin. We lost our office culture, but we replaced it with something stronger: a deep commitment to a culture of personal growth and development. We could not have done this without our mission, vision, and values.

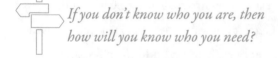 *If you don't know who you are, then how will you know who you need?*

# WHAT'S YOUR MISSION?

Your *mission* keeps you focused on what's most important. It is the core of who you are. It's critical for your team. It's your (and their) identity. It is your purpose for being.

If you want to find your mission, follow your passion.

Think about what you love about your business and how it serves the greater good. Do you help people start their days right, like a coffee shop? Do you protect people from the unexpected, like an insurance company? Do you help families enjoy time in their homes, like a housekeeping service?

I've always had a passion for helping people find their callings in life. I am the person friends call when they need career advice or help with their resumes. So, that's where I focused when I decided to start a business. Let's just say that it wasn't a straight line to success.

My first business idea was a resume writing service. I didn't do anything other than give it a name (Resume Architects) and create a crummy logo in Microsoft Word. Later on, I came up with a rule that I only wanted to run a business that served customers with 1) money and 2) ongoing needs for our service. Resume Architects violated both of these rules: I was providing a one-time service for people who were most likely unemployed!

My next business idea had more of a marketing angle: I wanted to create websites to give job seekers an authentic view of what it was like to work for a company. This business got as far as a name (Company Camera), another crummy logo, *and* a bloated business plan. But it never launched. Companies told me that it sounded cool, but they were not sure about the value of it. One thing was clear: everyone wanted to attract more applicants. So, that's where I focused.

I took my company website idea and pivoted it into a candidate lead-generation service. I would send personalized microsites about specific career opportunities to qualified job seekers online. I called it CareerPlug because I wanted to focus on the connection between candidates and the right jobs. (That, and the careerplug. com domain name was available!)

A few years later, CareerPlug was helping large organizations generate applicants around the country. But I felt disconnected from my original passion. We worked for recruiters who simply needed us to feed their hiring machines with more leads.

I became intrigued by the idea of transforming us into a software company. I was particularly interested in helping small business owners with hiring. I saw how hard it was to balance running the business and running a hiring process at the same time—especially when you were short-staffed! I knew there had to be a better way to do it, and I decided that we were up for the challenge.

We became a software company that helps thousands of companies hire the right people, and that passion grew into CareerPlug's mission: Make hiring easier.

Over time, we realized that our clients needed our help beyond hiring. To help them succeed, they needed to improve their employee retention. We believe that the best way to retain people long-term is to help them grow and reach their potential in their careers. So we updated our mission to reflect that: Empower people to reach their potential. This was an important statement to make to our team and clients, and it has helped guide the decisions we make throughout the organization.

Our mission guides everything that we do. It keeps us motivated and focused. If something doesn't make hiring easier, then we should not do it. It also helps us hire and retain the talent that fuels our growth. We help small businesses grow and help people find the right jobs. Our team loves this. It inspires them to help the company succeed much more than if we were simply chasing profits.

People are attracted to businesses that serve purposes higher than their own. It may not be what you think about running the business day-to-day, but it is important to stay connected to your mission and passion. After all, isn't that why you got into this business in the first place?

 *If you stripped away everything else, what is your one reason for being in business?*

# WHERE ARE YOU HEADED?

Once you know your purpose—your mission—you need to define where you're going and who you want to be. That's your *vision*. People often confuse the two. Your mission is who you are. Your vision is where you are headed—it is who you want to become.

I've believed in visualizing my future ever since I read *Think and Grow Rich* by Napoleon Hill. After reading it, I wrote "I am going to start a business" on an index card and taped it to the bathroom mirror in my apartment. I read it every morning and evening while I brushed my teeth. I guess that was the first version of our vision statement.

Once CareerPlug began to grow, I updated the vision statement to a new sentence. It wasn't memorable or particularly inspiring—something like "Become the leader in hiring software for our target markets." Then I read *Vivid Vision* by Cameron Herold, and it changed my perspective. I wrote a three-page vision statement that described, in detail, the kind of company that we would be three years down the road.

Our vision focuses on the *what*, as in *what is going to happen?* It does not spell out how we will get there. That is what we get to work on together as a team each day over the course of three years. And when those three years are up, we create a new version for the next three years. High performers love this. They want a leader to point them in the right direction and then get out of the way. By giving your team the vision but not the solution, you show that you trust them to figure it out. They want this challenge and the satisfaction of achieving the goal.

We now share our vision statement with candidates before they interview with us. It is amazing how they react. The best candidates have been craving to be part of something special, something bigger than themselves. They read it and come back to us with lots of questions. This is a great sign: I love to hire curious people. Other candidates fade away. This is a gift, a potentially bad hire avoided.

 *Are you and your team clear on where you're headed?*

# WHAT DO YOU VALUE?

Your *core values* signify what you, as a company, prize more than anything. They should guide everything that you do. If you are not sure about what direction to head in a tough situation, you should be able to look at your values to determine the right course of action.

You should be hiring, developing, promoting, and firing people based on your values. If you're not, then you're not truly living them.

A company's values are a reflection of its leader. You cannot lead others if you do not know who you are. And you cannot expect others to follow you unless this is crystal clear.

This bears repeating: your values should represent what you *actually* value. They define your culture. We have all been somewhere where they have a generic set of values printed and framed on the wall. You know that they are totally bogus and that no one follows them—or even knows what they are!

It's better to be real, even if you don't think your values sound socially acceptable. If earning money is the #1 thing for you and your company, then you should be honest about that. There are people out there who value the same things, and those are the people you want to hire.

Part of being real is having values with character. They need to be genuine and come from the heart. We value teamwork at Career-Plug, but that term didn't capture the essence of it. So, we came up with our own: *Work Together, Win Together*. I hear people say this throughout the company when we talk about the importance of collaboration. I don't think that "teamwork" would have stuck the same way as a core value.

Your values should reflect who you are *right now*. When you write your values, you should be drawing from your history; save the aspirational stuff for your vision. We decided to include *Speak Up, Step Up* as one of our values because we have always valued people who are willing to take initiative. We have a history of allowing people to take on special projects at the company simply because they've shown a strong desire to make an impact in a certain area. It wasn't just a goal—we were already living it.

Don't make a laundry list of values. When you "value" everything, you really value nothing.

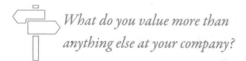 *What do you value more than anything else at your company?*

# OUR VALUES BREAKDOWN

Once we had our mission, vision, and values written, we had so much more clarity as an organization. But I still felt like there was something missing: a way to determine the traits that I wanted every single person in CareerPlug to embody.

A few years later, I felt like our culture took a turn for the worse. We made some hires that were not a good culture fit for us, and there were consequences. We became more divided as a company, and each department started to operate in its own silo. Something had to change.

I knew we had to address the situation with certain employees at the company. That was tough but fairly straightforward. I was more concerned about how we were going to prevent ourselves from hiring people who were not a culture fit in the future.

Our core values should have been helping us, but they weren't. I identified three issues:

1.  We had too many values. There were seven of them. There was no way that our team could focus on seven different things when evaluating candidates in the hiring process on top of evaluating them for their fit for the role itself. Plus, it's hard to make any core value non-negotiable when you have seven of them. If someone is living six out of the seven values, doesn't that sound good enough? It does, and that was the problem.

2. Some of our values did not have clearly defined boundaries. For example, most of the emphasis on our *Give Back* core value was focused on a candidate's time spent giving to external charities. But that value was also meant to cover how a person approaches giving their time to others within the company. It was too much.

3. The values didn't nail what truly makes our employees a culture fit. I actually added a list of four additional items, which I called *culture drivers,* to address this gap. It helped in some ways, but it was a band-aid. We should have rewritten the values to reflect what really matters.

It took longer than it should have, but that's what we eventually did.

 *How well do your values help you hold people accountable to being a fit for your culture?*

# GETTING VALUES RIGHT

We identified our new core values based on a process that Patrick Lencioni recommends in his book, *The Advantage*.

First, we had each person on the leadership team identify the top performers at the company who truly embody our culture. Then we asked each leader to list out the behaviors or attributes that made these individuals so respected. These became our potential core values. We wrote this list on a whiteboard without discussing any individual employees by name. There were around fifteen to twenty potential core values to start.

Then, we went through the list and discussed each value as a team. After eliminating a few and consolidating some that were similar, we were left with around eight values.

Next, we asked each leader to think about the employees, both current and former, who were not a good fit at our company—regardless of how well they performed in their roles. Then, we had our leaders assess these individuals on the list of remaining core values. We identified a couple of core values that, while important, didn't do a good enough job of excluding people who were not a good culture fit. We eliminated them from the list, leaving us with six values.

Finally, we reviewed the remaining values and thought deeply about what was really true to us at our core. We eliminated one value that was too aspirational and another that wasn't as important as the rest. That left us with the four core values we have today:

Be Kind

Speak Up, Step Up

Keep Growing

Work Together, Win Together

I knew that these were genuine because I had a backstory that I could tell for each one.

## BE KIND

My employees would tell you that I'm a nice person. I don't like to work with people who aren't. Neither does the rest of our team. When we dug deeper into it, we discovered that we value something more than "nice"—we value kindness. We look for people who care deeply about each other, our clients, and the world around us. We realized that we are givers, and it's a lot more fun to work with givers than takers!

## SPEAK UP, STEP UP

We have always valued people who take initiative, and we give them the room to do it. One of our long-time employees, Anna, read our vision and was energized by our commitment to give back to the environment. She took the initiative to create a sustainability committee, which has been a big hit with our team. Within a couple of months, they implemented several programs to reduce our waste. This is one example of many situations where someone has stepped up. And when we reflected on employees who were not a fit, we realized that most of them had thoughts about things we could improve (and some were quite vocal about them)—but they didn't take action.

## KEEP GROWING

I didn't know much about hiring or software when I started CareerPlug, but I knew that I could make up for that by focusing on continuous learning and growth. We have always been attracted to hiring learners with high potential over people with more experience but a lower trajectory. This was solidified when I read Carol Dweck's *Mindset* and her research on people with fixed versus growth mindsets. We now do even more to encourage our employees' growth and promote from within whenever possible.

## WORK TOGETHER, WIN TOGETHER

We are a collaborative company. It's in our DNA: we ask for help, we help, we solve problems together. We put the good of the team and the company above our individual benefit. If you are a lone wolf or someone who puts your own interests first, then this isn't the place for you.

The lesson I learned is that simply having core values is not good enough. You must be able to use your core values to hire, develop, promote, and fire employees effectively. If you cannot, then

I recommend you follow a similar process to the one we used to reevaluate your values.

 *How do you use your core values to make key decisions?*

# MAKE IT MEMORABLE

Defining your mission, vision, and values will not be worth anything if you cannot get your team to live them every day. If you don't talk about them as a leader, they will accumulate dust and be forgotten.

Get your team involved in developing and documenting your culture. You cannot do it all yourself. You *shouldn't* do it all yourself. Your team will help you make sure that it is authentic. They will see your blind spots. Plus, you need them to buy into it, and there's no better way than to have them help you create it.

That being said, it still starts with you—no one knows the business better.

I spent a lot of time reflecting on what was most important to me and where I wanted to take the business. Then I wrote down everything in a rough draft and took it to my team so that we could refine it and make it *ours*.

*Make sure that people can see it.* We put our values on the wall, but not in a cheesy frame. We had a designer create a mural on the largest wall in the office with all of our values using our brand colors and imagery. I feel like our company (and our culture) took a big leap forward that day.

*Make sure that people can hear it and talk about it.* I learned a great way to incorporate this into our daily routine from one of our clients, Neighborly. They start each meeting of more than three people by reciting their core values as a team. This may seem elementary in some ways, but it works! Neighborly has been able to align a decentralized franchise system of over 2,000 independent owners into a high-performing culture that sets the standard in their industry. At CareerPlug, we now start each meeting by reciting our core values, so everyone on our team, even the newest employee, is on the same page with what we value most.

*Make sure that people know that you value it.* When managers make the case to hire someone for their team, they need to show everyone how the candidate fits our values and culture—but we do this for more than just hiring. Our core values are included in performance reviews for all team members; our leaders make a point of referencing specific ones when praising people and celebrating wins, and the rest of the team has followed suit. Each Friday afternoon, we do an all-hands meeting with the entire team, and the highlights are the *Shout Outs*, when team members recognize colleagues for doing something great. They often mention a specific value, which I love!

Remember that it starts with you as the leader. You show that you value something by talking about it, displaying it, and praising it. If you don't, no one else will.

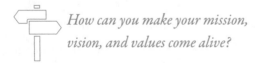 *How can you make your mission, vision, and values come alive?*

# WHETHER YOU CAN OR CANNOT

... you are probably right.

Running a business is tough. And it doesn't get much easier as you grow—there are just different sets of challenges. A lot of your success comes down to your mindset. Here are some common objections that I hear when I speak with people about creating their mission, vision, and values:

*I don't have the time.*

Time is about prioritization. You make time for things that are important to you. If you want to build a great company, then you need to make building a great team your priority. Creating your mission/vision/values requires deep thought, so it is best if you set aside a block of time (at least half a day) to work on this. You should get out of the office to avoid distractions. When it is time to involve your team, consider scheduling an offsite meeting, and if you can afford it, hire someone to facilitate so that you can fully participate. You will be amazed at how productive these can be. Don't have time during the workday? Do it one evening or over the weekend.

*I am part of a larger organization.*

If you are a leader within a large company or part of a franchise system, you still have the opportunity to create a mission, vision, and values for your team. It is important that yours align with the parent company's. Think of yours as an extension of theirs. Yes, you may be more restricted, but there was something about the organization that attracted you to it: Embrace that and build upon it.

*We are a very small business.*

If you only need to make one hire, constructing your mission/vision/values might seem like overkill. Maybe—but doesn't your size actually make that one hire that much *more* important? If you cannot show someone what you value and where you are headed, what kind of talent do you expect to attract? If you can only afford to make one hire, then you need to make it the best one possible. And the best way to do that is to create your mission, vision, and values—even just simplified versions. Aside from hiring, it will help you focus and run your business better. CareerPlug would have grown so much faster if I had done this sooner.

 *What belief is holding you back right now?*

# SHOW WHO YOU ARE

YOU ATTRACT WHO YOU ARE

WHY SHOULD I WORK FOR YOU?

RATE YOUR CAREERS PAGE

KEEP IT REAL

# YOU ATTRACT WHO YOU ARE

Who you are is your brand. Your brand attracts a certain type of customer. Your positioning in the market helps customers determine whether what you value aligns with what they value. Your brand is going to be a good match for some people and a bad one for others—and that's the whole point of branding. The more you fine-tune your brand and how you communicate it, the better you will be at attracting the right type of customer.

The same is true for your employees: **You attract people who value the same things that you do.**

I can see this throughout my company. I am entrepreneurial. I am a lifelong learner. I love to travel. I don't like to micromanage (or be micromanaged). As a result, I have attracted people who value these same things. Some people have come to work for us and learned that they value different things. They no longer work here.

This does not mean that everyone at CareerPlug is all the same. We are diverse in many ways. We have lots of different talents and skills, but our mission, vision, and values bring us together. Everyone here decided that they believe in who we are and where we are headed—and they want to be a part of it.

Whether you know it or not, you have an employer brand. Applicants may not know what it is, but your employees do. The clearer you can be about who you are and what you have to offer, the more attractive you will be to the right types of candidates for you.

*What type of applicants is your brand attracting right now?*

# WHY SHOULD I WORK FOR YOU?

Candidates may not ask you this question directly, but they are definitely asking themselves.

Job seekers have never had more choices. They can access millions of jobs from their phones and apply to many of them with just a few clicks. This has revolutionized searching for a job in the same way that online shopping changed the way we buy things.

Put yourself in a job seeker's shoes. What would you find if you researched your company online? Would you want to apply for a job at your company based on what you see? What story are you telling them? Are you telling them a story at all?

The first place people look is often your website's careers page. Your careers page is your opportunity to show why you are a great place to work. There are certain things that have universal appeal to high performers: The ability to learn and grow. The opportunity to make an impact. Flexibility. Great benefits. These are a start, but you can do better. Focus on what makes your company special—more specifically, what your top performers have told you makes it special.

You need to answer the questions that candidates are asking themselves, preferably with examples:

**Culture:** What's it like to work here? What are we like? Why do we love it?

**Compensation & Benefits:** How competitive is our compensation? What sort of perks do we offer?

**Growth:** How do we invest in training and development? How can employees grow with us?

It's not enough for *you* to know what makes your organization a great place to work. You have to show potential applicants! Better yet, your employees should show them.

Almost every candidate that we speak with says that they read reviews about us before applying or interviewing. Are you aware of how employees are talking about your company online? You should manage this the same way that you manage customer reviews. Encourage happy employees to leave reviews for you. Respond to reviews that are negative in a caring, non-defensive way. Don't make job seekers leave your website to look for reviews and ratings. Include them with other testimonials on your careers page.

Put the work into showing people why they should work for you. In addition to creating an attractive online presence, it will also give you and your team a consistent message to share with candidates throughout the hiring process.

 *What story is your online presence telling job seekers?*

# RATE YOUR CAREERS PAGE

Not all careers pages are created equal. Here is how I classify them:

**Level 0**: You don't have a careers page, or if you do have one, it is a bare minimum effort that usually has a general statement like, "We are always looking for good people," or "We value our people," that does nothing to show job seekers why. It does not list any specific job postings or descriptions. Normally there is a message to come apply in person or send your resume to a generic email address like jobs@yourcompany.com.

**Level 1**: This type of careers page often has a list of job openings, and that's about it. It doesn't provide job seekers with a good picture of what it's like to work there. There's little to no effort put into showing job seekers why this is a great place to work. You can usually apply to individual jobs, but the application process is long and generic.

**Level 2**: This type of careers page works harder to show why your company is a great place to work, but it usually does not prove it by letting a job seeker hear from employees. If there are photos on the site, they are most likely generic stock photos. There are specific jobs listed, but everything feels impersonal and corporate. And the application process is often long and not mobile-friendly.

**Level 3**: This is a compelling careers page. Not only is your company showcased as a great place to work, but the page gives job seekers a genuine feel for what it's like to work there. There are photos of actual employees, and even employee testimonials and videos. These pages also share your mission and core values. The right people feel an immediate connection, and they are excited about the opportunity to join the team. You make it easy for them to find your open positions and apply to any job within minutes. This is the type of careers page you need.

When I ask some of our employees why they applied to work at CareerPlug, they say things like:

> *"After looking at your careers page, I could just see myself working here and making friends."*
>
> *"I loved reading about your core values. There was definitely a connection."*
>
> *"CareerPlug was different from other places I looked. I could tell that there was something special happening here."*

Don't let a Level 0–2 effort keep you from attracting top performers who would otherwise love to work for you.

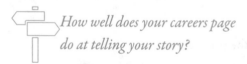 *How well does your careers page do at telling your story?*

Check out our *Compelling Careers Page Checklist* on **howtohire.com**

# KEEP IT REAL

Be authentic about who you are as a company, and you will attract the right kind of people.

CareerPlug competes with large, well-funded tech companies with appealing perks and ongoing needs for talent. There are also high-flying startups that have raised venture capital and offer the potential for a big payday if everything works out as planned. Highly skilled tech workers have no shortage of opportunities, and we have to work hard to stand out from the crowd as a boot-strapped company.

How do we do it?

- We embrace the things that make us different from the larger tech companies and high-flying startups. We are a well-established, profitable company. At the same time, we don't have outside investors influencing our actions. This is a sweet spot for our team. Our employees don't want to get lost in Corporate America, but they also want less risk and a better work/life balance than most startups offer.
- We talk about the potential to make a real impact for our company and our clients. We make software that helps companies grow their teams with the right people. As a result, a lot of people get new jobs—well over 100,000 of them each year!

- We speak frankly about our culture and the advantages/disadvantages that come along with joining a team like ours. For example, we are a highly collaborative company. If you are more of a lone wolf who likes to work solo, then we are not the right place for you.
- We walk the walk by pursuing our mission and living our values every day.

We know from experience that hiring people who are genuinely excited to contribute to the growth of a company like ours is the most important indicator of success for new hires.

But remember: it's more important to actually *be* a great place to work than it is to promote yourself as one. If you promise candidates something but don't deliver on it, the truth will come out. It's very easy for a current or former employee to leave a review that will live on the internet forever.

The lesson I've learned is that if you are authentic about who you are and how you showcase your company, you will attract candidates who are right for you. When you promote your company as something that it is not, you will attract the wrong type of people. They will figure it out and leave.

Or worse, they will stay.

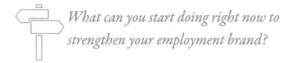

*What can you start doing right now to strengthen your employment brand?*

RECRUIT

# KNOW WHO YOU NEED

PEOPLE FIRST

RIGHT SEATS

START WITH YOUR SEAT

RIGHT PEOPLE ON

WRONG PEOPLE OFF

IDEAL CANDIDATE PROFILE

INVEST IN YOUR GROWTH

EVERY HIRE COUNTS

# PEOPLE FIRST

There are three essential components of a successful business: strategy, people, and process. Someone once asked me which one was most important, and my mind immediately went to Jim Collins. Here's how he put it in *Good to Great*:

> *The executives who ignited the transformations from good to great did not first figure out where to drive the bus and then get people to take it there. No, they first got the right people on the bus (and the wrong people off the bus) and then figured out where to drive it. They said, in essence, 'Look, I don't really know where we should take this bus. But I know this much: If we get the right people on the bus, the right people in the right seats, and the wrong people off the bus, then we'll figure out how to take it someplace great.'*

I hired my first employee, Garrett, about nine months after I started CareerPlug. His job title was intern, even though he'd graduated from the University of Texas a few years earlier. He worked in my apartment and did whatever it took to help me: Nights. Weekends. He would even take my dog for a walk when I was too busy! Talk about commitment. Garrett remained at the company for over twelve years, ascending all the way to Senior Director of Finance & Administration.

I hired David a couple of years after Garrett. He was another UT graduate who took a job as an intern, even though I needed him to work a full-time schedule (sometimes more). A few years into it, David took it upon himself to join a software development bootcamp to learn how to write code. He was interested in that type of work, and he knew that we needed it. David grew to be our Senior Director of Product.

We joke about the "internship program" now, but it played an important role when we got started. I was looking for people without egos who were willing to work hard, and that job title weeded out a lot of people. I chose to hire people with the right character and drive versus the right experience. Too often, companies overlook character to hire someone with the right experience. This is almost always a mistake.

We did not figure out that we were going to become a hiring software company until well after Garrett and David joined us. We got the right people on the bus, then we figured out where to take it. We would not be where we are today without those two.

Focus on people first. These early hires will set the trajectory for your business.

 *Who are the key players on the bus with you?*

# RIGHT SEATS

The best way to determine if you have the right seats on your bus is to look at where you are right now and where you are headed.

Start by drawing your current org chart. Don't do this on your computer—use a sheet of paper or a whiteboard. If you have a smaller company, include all roles. If you are larger, start with your leadership team and work your way down to a level that makes sense. But don't list any names on the seats yet—that will come later.

For each seat, list the job functions that this seat carries. This may include key functions for this role, as well as some things that the person in this role happens to carry (this is especially common in small businesses where people have to wear many hats).

Now take a moment to process what you see. What do you like and not like about it? What do you think about the roles? Do they make sense, or would it make more sense to organize the functions a different way?

Now, think about the future that you envision for the business and draw a separate *future org chart*. I like to look ahead three years, but looking ahead one year may be a good start if you are still working in the business. Your vision statement should guide you. What will your team need to look like to support the kind of business that you envision? Start at the top and work your way down to the appropriate level. Focus on the roles and the functions that each role will carry before you write down any people's names.

Once you have the roles identified and the reporting structure organized, you can start thinking about your current team and adding names to roles. You should also identify people who may not have a future at the company.

Take some time to compare the two org charts and get feedback from your coach or advisors. This should help you answer some key questions:

- *Which roles will need to change?*
- *Which roles will need to be added?*
- *Which people will be staying put, moving up, or moving out?*

Often, I have found that looking at the future this way helps me see the present more clearly. Sometimes these are not changes that need to happen in the future—they need to happen *right now*. The future org chart allows you to spot opportunities more quickly. It can lead you to create a job post for a key growth position or to identify a potential candidate that you might have otherwise overlooked. It also may be the wake-up call that you need to have a difficult conversation that you have put off.

# START WITH YOUR SEAT

The first seat that you should look at is your own.

As a business grows, the leader's role shifts away from doing work to running the business. Michael Gerber talks about this shift in *The E-Myth Revisited*. He coined the phrase, "Working on the business, not in the business." This is an important shift that leaders must make, as your business will never reach its full potential until you make this transition.

When I first started CareerPlug, we were not even a software company. We provided a recruitment marketing service, sourcing qualified resumes and contacting job seekers on behalf of certain employers. And it wasn't "we"—it was just me. I had to do everything, and I worked nonstop. I did not hire my first employee until my wife forced me to. I had made the mistake of working in bed (never a good idea for your relationship), and she said, "Give me your computer." She went to Craigslist and posted a job for me.

When I hired Garrett, I got some relief, which gave me time to work on our first software application (an internal tool to help us manage all of the resumes we sourced and people we contacted). This allowed us to handle a lot more business, but I was still working a ton and most of it was in the business. When I hired a second employee, David, he relieved me from my "night job" of reviewing resumes, and I was able to focus on selling to new accounts. I also started to work on the business and think about the future of CareerPlug.

I knew that I wanted to evolve from a service business to a software business. More specifically, I wanted to build software that helped businesses hire great people. I just needed to figure out how to do it. I got my chance when one of our clients, a large insurance company, asked if we could provide our resume-sourcing service for its network of independent agents. I worked with them to build an applicant tracking system for small business owners. I would have missed this opportunity if I had still been looking at resumes all day and night.

Even after this transition to software, my plate was full of lots of in-the-business functions. I was the only person doing sales at the company, and I was working hard to expand our software to other organizations. I hired our first sales representative, Brad, and he quickly went to work adding new clients for us at a much faster pace.

Once I gave up my sales function, most of my remaining functions involved managing others. It was still way too much for me to manage well; my future org chart (at that time) made it clear to me that I was going to be a bottleneck to our growth. So I updated our org chart and organized our people into teams. For certain teams, I was able to develop current team members into leaders and managers. I decided to hire outside managers to lead and grow other teams where we did not have the right person internally.

**Looking back, we took a leap forward every time I gave away one of my functions to someone more talented in that area.**

Someone once told me that there is an inverse relationship between growth and control. You can control everything, but you won't grow. Or you can give up control of everything and then grow out of control. The sweet spot falls somewhere between those two extremes and is different for each person. You get to decide.

*What do you need to give up to grow?*

Growth cannot happen unless you have the leaders under you to support it. Many decentralized businesses run into this issue; for example, they cannot open additional stores without people who can step up as leaders for those new locations (and other people who will step up to fill their shoes at the current locations). Don't let this be what holds you back from growing.

And don't get discouraged if your business isn't growing fast enough to support additional leaders yet. This growth often happens over a long period of time. It took me over ten years. Look for small steps you can take now.

Your goal should be to clear off the non-essential stuff from each plate and allow every person to spend more time on their *superpower*—starting with you. Your superpower is the intersection of your natural talents and passion. It's probably what got you into the role you're in today.

I spent way too many years doing our bookkeeping, even though I hated it, because I have an accounting degree. There are services out there that will be able to perform these functions for you at a higher quality and lower cost than you can. The outside bookkeeper did more than give me hours back to my month—he also helped me boost my energy level and focus on what I do best.

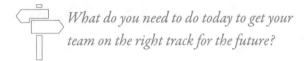 *What do you need to do today to get your team on the right track for the future?*

The first step to getting the right people on the bus is to evaluate who you currently have aboard. I do this by calculating a *Talent GPA* for my team. All that you need to do is ask a single question for each member of your team, and then grade your response:

*How would you feel if you found out that [EMPLOYEE NAME] was leaving the company?*

Here's the grading scale: (Note: This is a simple way to calculate the GPA. It may be more accurate for you to overweight the grades for leaders and other key roles.)

**A (4 points)** – Sudden feeling of being punched in the gut. You rush to the door to block it and try to do whatever you can to keep this person. You know that it's going to be a big hit to the team, and it will be hard to replace this person with someone as good.

**B (3 points)** – Disappointment and some concern about the short term. After getting past that, a feeling that you could, at the very least, hire someone as good—possibly better.

**C (2 points)** – Sudden feeling of relief and lightness. You rush to the door to open it and bid them farewell, knowing that you just received a golden opportunity to upgrade.

**F (0 points)** – Don't let the door hit you on the way out! (Note: If you have anyone on your team that is an F player, put this book aside *right now*—you need to remove this person from your team immediately. Every day that you keep them on, you are putting your company at risk of becoming toxic and losing your top performers.)

Be sure to factor in an employee's culture fit when assigning grades. Someone won't get an A from me unless they exemplify our values, no matter how good they are at their job. I have let some talented people go who were toxic to our culture. While their contributions were missed in some ways, I still felt relieved when they left (which meant their grade was no higher than a C).

If you are stuck between two grades for someone, ask yourself who does most of the pushing in the relationship? A Players make you think, *Wow. I really need to step up my game to lead this person.* That's them pushing you. C Players make you think, *Wow. This person doesn't get much done without me pushing them to do it.* B Players are somewhere in between. They take care of their work on their own, but you don't feel the pressure to improve like you do with an A Player.

The easiest way to calculate your Talent GPA is to start with an employee list with columns for grade and grade points. Then simply work your way down the list and enter a grade and the corresponding number of grade points for each employee. Finally, average all of the grade points.

Pay close attention to the grades of your leaders. Leaders and managers rarely build (and keep) a team with a Talent GPA higher than their own, so don't expect your B Player leader to build a team full of A Players. The quality of your leadership team will determine your company's trajectory and ultimate success. One of my mentors once showed me a simple org chart with a top leader and five direct reports. He told me, "This could be a six-person or 6,000-person organization. It all depends on the quality of your leadership team."

Ineffective leaders and managers do not just underperform—they can also drive away high performers. I believe the old saying, "People don't leave companies, they leave their managers." Be aware of this risk and take the appropriate actions.

In addition to tracking the grades on a spreadsheet, I print our org chart and write the grades next to each person's box. Then I try to take a step back mentally and look for insights. The visual aspect of the org chart has been so valuable to me. I have been able to spot issues and opportunities by looking at my team this way.

You can also conduct this exercise with your leaders and managers. Give them a copy of their team's org chart and ask them to write a grade next to each person based on how they would feel if their employee left. Check for alignment with your own thoughts. If this is an underperforming team and the manager does not identify any C's in the group, then they may be the C.

 *Who are the employees that drive your growth, and who are the ones that hold you back?*

Check out our *Talent GPA* exercise on **howtohire.com**

Once you have the grades for your employees, it's not as easy as keeping some on the bus and kicking others off. You should determine a course of action for each person. Consider working with each employee to develop growth plans that factor in their goals and a path they can take at the company. Here's some guidance on how to approach each group.

## B PLAYERS

I want to start with B Players because this should be the largest group of people on your team. If you rated almost every employee at your company as an A Player, take another look. Even if you do have above-average talent across the board at your company, you should have a top 10%–20% of your employees that stand out as the highest performers. They are your A Players. Likewise, your bottom 10%–20% should stand out as C Players. The rest are B Players (relatively speaking).

The most important thing that I have learned about B Players is this: **Their performance will move up when they are working with A Players and down when they are working with C Players.**

The best things that you can do for B Players is to:

1. Maximize the number of A Players on the team,
2. Minimize the number of C Players, and
3. Encourage their development and help them find their strength zones.

Something else to consider: I have seen B Players make the jump to the A level after a role change in the company (or after they got a new leader).

## A PLAYERS

The best things that you can do for A Players are to:

1. Take care of them with recognition and compensation, and
2. Remove obstacles so they can grow/thrive.

A Players outperform the rest of your team and should be rewarded accordingly. Remember that not all of them are motivated primarily by money. Make sure that you know what's most important to them (development, achievement, recognition, compensation) and focus on helping them get what they want. Understand what they want to accomplish in their careers, and clear the path for them to achieve it. If you don't do this, they will look for it somewhere else.

The easiest way to lose an A Player is to surround them with C Players. A friend of mine once told me that "Eagles don't like to fly with crows." I don't think that I can put it any better than that.

## C PLAYERS

With this group, you need to get them moving up or moving out. Ask yourself why these people are underperforming and develop performance improvement plans for them. Are they in the wrong role or with the wrong manager? Is there something happening in their lives affecting their performance? Is this a character issue? Do I see a path to get these people to become B Players (or higher)?

You owe it to these people to communicate any performance issues and develop action plans to improve their performance. If you don't do this, then you are not only letting these people down as their leader—you are letting down the rest of your team. Grades and people can change. It's your job to put them in the best positions to succeed. If you need to part ways with them, you will have done it the right way.

Carrying the burden of an underperformer may hurt more than you think. In some cases, a team can produce more without that person, even if they are not replaced. How is that possible? Think about a sales team: The underperformer may be squandering solid leads that another rep would close. The leader of the team may need to spend a disproportionate amount of time on the under-performer, time that's taken away from more productive reps and their deals. Worst of all, morale decreases and the standard for performance falls.

One additional thought on this group: Kim Scott (author of *Radical Candor*) gave me a new perspective on underperformers. She says that most people have the potential to be A Players if they are put in the right roles. Is there another type of role that may suit your underperformer better? If this role exists at the company, then you should explore it. If not, you may not be doing this person a favor by keeping them. You may be keeping them from becoming an A Player somewhere else.

I have never made the mistake of letting someone go too soon. When I think about the times I've had to fire people, my regrets are that 1) I should have given them more feedback, and 2) I should have acted sooner.

## DON'T COMPROMISE ON CHARACTER

I look for three things in a candidate: ability, motivation, and culture fit. You can train someone on ability and work with them if they are not performing, but you cannot compromise on motivation or culture fit. If someone is not willing to put in the hours and work hard for you, don't give them another minute of your time. If someone is not aligned with your company's core values, you need to get them off the bus. Too many leaders overlook character issues if a person is a high performer. This is a huge mistake. If you don't get this person off the bus, then you may lose your best performers—the ones who embody your core values.

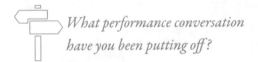 *What performance conversation have you been putting off?*

Check out our *Performance Improvement Plan* template on **howtohire.com**

# IDEAL CANDIDATE PROFILE

Once you have evaluated what you can give away and your future org chart, it should be easier to identify who is missing and which roles need to be filled. Before you rush to post a job, it's helpful to get organized. You need to understand the role that needs to be filled and the type of person you need to fill it. And you need to document it so you can hold yourself accountable during the hiring process.

We do this by using a planning tool called an *Ideal Candidate Profile*. The Ideal Candidate Profile helps you identify the key function for the role and the qualifications for a top performer.

There are four sections of the Ideal Candidate Profile:

1. Background
2. Key Function
3. Responsibilities
4. Qualifications

## BACKGROUND

We start our planning process by answering some questions to make sure we understand our current needs. We didn't always have this section. It got added after I was asked to approve some new hires, and the hiring managers didn't have clear answers when I asked them these questions. Even if you are the hiring manager, it's important to consider these questions before diving into a hiring process.

- Briefly describe the role you want to fill.
- Why do we need this role?
- Why is now the time to hire for this role?
- What are the costs/risks if we choose not to hire for this role?

## KEY FUNCTION

Before you dive into all of the tasks that you want this person to perform, start by identifying the key function that you need performed in the role. What metric or result will this person be responsible for producing? This role could have more than one key function, but be careful not to turn this into a laundry list. Focus on the one or two key functions that you need this person to perform well. If this is a new role for you, search for similar jobs online to see which tasks and responsibilities are listed—or speak with someone in your network who has someone in this type of role on their team.

## RESPONSIBILITIES

List out the tasks that need to be performed on a daily, weekly, monthly, and quarterly basis to support this role's key function(s). Then add any other responsibilities that you expect this person to carry. Take a step back and review the list. Would performing these tasks well lead to producing the key metric or result that you desire? Does it feel like too much, too little, or just right? If there is too much, then you may need to revisit the scope of the key function(s). If it's too little, think about what else this person could carry or whether you need to hire anyone at all.

In my experience, hiring managers are more likely to give someone too many responsibilities versus not enough. The risk here is that you dilute this person's contribution toward what really matters.

## QUALIFICATIONS

Once you have the functions documented, your next step is to identify the *talents*, *skills*, and *behaviors* you would expect to see in a top performer.

**Talents** are natural, inherited aspects of someone's aptitude. Someone's talents can be tied to their personality—they could be friendly and outgoing, or cautious and analytical. Other talents could be related to someone's natural cognitive or physical ability.

**Skills** are developed abilities learned through education and experience. They can show whether a person can perform a specific function competently. Certain talents may give a person an advantage in developing a skill, but talents are not a replacement for skills. Someone will still need to learn how to perform a task or function.

**Behaviors** are the ways in which someone conducts themselves, especially toward others. Behaviors reflect someone's attitude, which can reveal workplace preferences. For example, a person may prefer to work alone rather than in a collaborative environment. That is important to know if the role requires someone to work with others frequently.

How will you know whether someone possesses the talents, skills, and behaviors you need? You should note how you plan to measure each talent, skill, and behavior you list. This step will help you later as you organize your hiring process.

Talents and behaviors are best measured through personality assessments and structured interviews. It's important that a person's talents and behaviors match up with the role. It takes a lot of energy to perform a function if it does not come naturally to you. In my experience, people can do almost any kind of function in the short term. They may not do it well, but they will work hard at it. Over time, this wears you out and saps your motivation. When a better opportunity comes along that matches your personality, you will be gone.

My wife likes to remind me of this point all the time. She jokes with me about all of the professions that I would fail at; one of them is as an attorney. I test high for agreeableness and generally avoid conflict when I can. I am persuasive and could do well in a debate if needed, but it would wear me out. I would not last long in that profession!

Skills are best measured through interviewing, particularly with interviews that allow candidates to demonstrate their skills. It's important to not automatically take experience as skill. Someone could have been a customer service representative for a year, but that does not necessarily mean that he has the skills you need. He could have been a poor performer. Or he could have worked at a company with low standards and a different definition of customer service than yours.

It can be difficult to pinpoint the right talents and skills, particularly the talents. Study your top performers. Give them personality assessments for further insight. You can also give the same assessment to your average team members to provide perspective on how your top performers stand apart.

Remember that quality beats quantity. There are certain things that you will look for in any person you hire. You will naturally look for things like goal orientation, team player mentality, and strong communication skills when you evaluate someone—they don't belong in your Ideal Candidate Profile. Focus on what will separate the top performers from the rest of the pack.

Planning for a hire takes work to do right. But it will pay off. It will be so much easier to write your job description once you have an Ideal Candidate Profile. And you will increase your likelihood of attracting and selecting a top performer (and avoiding a bad hire). I think that Abraham Lincoln said it best: "Give me six hours to chop down a tree, and I will spend the first four sharpening the axe."

 *How clear are you on who you really need for a role?*

---

Check out our *Ideal Candidate Profile* template on **howtohire.com**

---

Once you identify who you need, you're going to experience a pause as a leader. This might be a brief pause if you need to replace someone (or if you are completely drowning in work), but there will be a pause. And a question: *Do I really need to add another person to the team (and the payroll)?*

You need to think about adding people to your team as an investment in the growth of your business; it needs to be the right time, the right position, and the right person. You won't have clear answers to these things unless you are clear on where you want to take the business: This is where you need your vision to guide you.

I have needed to expand my vision to make room for the talent that I have attracted. I always knew that I did not want to have a huge company or raise money from outside investors. There is nothing wrong with those aspirations; they just weren't for me. It was not too long ago that I thought $1 million in revenue was the most I could ever make in a year: it might as well have been all the money in the world.

Then one day, a mentor drew a circle and put me in the middle, then told me, "This represents everything that you need. But if you want to attract real talent, you need to keep drawing bigger circles to make room for everyone else and their own circles."

This made so much sense to me. I used to think that setting huge financial goals was selfish and greedy. It's actually the opposite. Now, I am motivated to help my team achieve their goals and prosperity. I love to see our team members driving new cars and hear about homes they have purchased. It shows that they are confident in their roles and with our company.

Making that investment in their business and in their people is probably one of the biggest hurdles that owners face to growth. I don't think it's a good idea to hire people too far ahead of growth. This can get you into trouble. When we get busy, I like to stretch the team some, to test our true capacity. These are important moments that often produce innovation. People figure out how to work smarter; certain tasks are suddenly not that important, and they are eliminated or perhaps automated. We also want to see whether this busy period is a blip or if it will be sustained in the longer term. (You will be able to tell the difference.) Be careful not to stretch your team for too long, though. Otherwise, it will burn people out and they will leave, killing the momentum that you worked so hard to build.

I make two exceptions to my rule on not hiring ahead of growth: 1) hiring a sales rep to produce the growth and 2) hiring someone to take part of my job from me. I am not a gambler, but if I had to bet on anyone or anything, it would be on myself. You won't grow until you invest in your growth, and when you hire someone to take a less important function away from you, you are betting on your ability to turn that time you gained into fuel for business growth. That can come from new ideas, improved strategies, or just more focused leadership.

*What are you willing to invest in your growth?*

# EVERY HIRE COUNTS

Every time you make a hire, you will either increase or decrease your Talent GPA. This becomes tougher to control as you grow because you have less direct involvement in each hire. Many fast-growing companies have been derailed because of poor hiring decisions made by managers.

**The best way to increase your Talent GPA over time is to develop an effective hiring system.**

An effective hiring system includes processes to:

1. Attract qualified applicants
2. Make better hiring decisions
3. Onboard and retain new hires successfully

Your hiring system needs to be a playbook with documented processes that you and your team can use to produce predictable results. It took me years to get my team there, and we learned a lot of hard lessons along the way. In the rest of this book, I'll share those lessons with you and help you create the hiring playbook you need to grow your business.

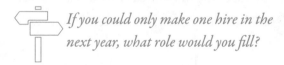

*If you could only make one hire in the next year, what role would you fill?*

# RECRUIT LIKE YOU SELL

GREAT CUSTOMER OR GREAT EMPLOYEE?

CREATE AN ATTRACTIVE JOB POSTING

BUILD YOUR LEAD GENERATION SYSTEM

START WITH EMPLOYEE REFERRALS

TELL YOUR CUSTOMERS & NETWORK

WIN ON THE JOB BOARDS

HOW MUCH IS A GREAT HIRE WORTH?

MAKE IT EASY TO APPLY!

SPEED AND PERSISTENCE WIN

ALWAYS BE RECRUITING

# GREAT CUSTOMER OR GREAT EMPLOYEE?

Which one would you rather have?

When I ask leaders this question, they almost always realize that a great employee is much more valuable. I use the word *realize* because I often see a light bulb flash as they answer.

Top performers are multipliers for your business. They thrill your customers and keep them coming back for more. One employee could help you produce dozens or even hundreds of new customers. Plus, they raise your Talent GPA and help you attract other top performers.

Poor hires will do the exact opposite. They will drive away your customers and your top performers.

Think about the best employee you have ever had. Consider the impact this person made. You are probably smiling right now, just thinking about it. What would you be willing to do to attract more of that kind of talent?

Now think about the worst one. Ouch. I just did the same thing. Smile: gone. What would you be willing to do to avoid repeating that pain?

So why don't we pursue great employees like we do great customers?

You need to recruit them. And you need to recruit like you sell.

Why do most companies fail to recruit the way they sell? The best practices that have made them successful in sales are nowhere to be seen in their recruiting process. *No value proposition. No easy way to get started. No follow-up.* You would never let this fly with your sales. Processes would be built. New standards and goals would be introduced. People would be held accountable to results. And the results would be there.

*How would your business change if you treated recruiting as your most important sale?*

# CREATE AN ATTRACTIVE JOB POSTING

You have put work into knowing who you are and what you need. Now it's time to create the job posting that will attract the right applicants. First, you need to create the content—then you need to promote it.

When I first got into the recruiting industry, it was common for job postings to focus only on the requirements for the job. These postings were sometimes referred to as *requisitions*, which are supposed to be internal documents to request hires. After these new hires were approved, people simply took the requisition document and turned it into a job posting. It was all about what the company needed and nothing else. And it annoyed me so much!

Imagine if you did this in your advertisements for customers. Is hiring really that different? You are not going to attract top performers unless you understand what they want and show them how they can get it with you.

I look for three things in an effective job posting:

## EASY TO FIND & READ
Make the posting easy to find by using the right job title and including the appropriate keywords throughout the description. If you do this right, then you will get lots of visibility on job boards. Research your job title on job boards to see what other jobs show

up. This will help you determine whether you are on the right track, and it may also help you identify some keywords to include in your description. Be sure to include information about the job location, job type (full-time/part-time), and compensation. Most job boards allow job seekers to filter results by these fields, so it is important to include them.

Once someone starts reading your job posting, it should be easy to navigate. This means clear sections with headers. The sections that we typically use are company overview, position overview, responsibilities, qualifications, benefits, and next steps. Avoid using big blocks of text or too many bullets. If you list every little thing that you want in a candidate, then they will miss out on what is most important to you.

You may not have a problem rattling off all of the tasks that you need this hire to do in a day, but can you give them the big picture of what you want them to accomplish in the role and why that is important to your company? This is what top performers care about.

After you have written the job posting, email it to yourself and review it from your phone (not your computer), since this is where most of your applicants will see it. How does it make you feel? Does it feel like one of those emails that makes you go "Ugh," or is it more like, "Ah, no problem!" Aim for the latter. You don't need to make the job sound easy, but it should be easy to understand.

## EXCITES THE RIGHT CANDIDATES

The right candidates should get excited as they read your job posting. They should be thinking, "Wow, this might be the one!" Tell them about your company, your mission, and your culture. Let them know why people love working there. Give the job posting some personality. Use a voice and tone that is in line with how you communicate internally. If your culture is more casual, don't write a job posting that makes you sound more formal.

Present them with a challenge. Talk about your mission and the specific challenge that you want the person in this position to solve. Let them know that you need their help.

Show them what's in it for them. Start with compensation and benefits. Be as open about these things as possible. Don't stop there. What else do they get? What are those perks that your top employees love? Take time to spell out all of the benefits in detail.

## CLEAR QUALIFICATIONS & NEXT STEPS

Be clear about what you need for the role, but be careful about what you list as required. I have worked with many leaders who listed five years of experience as a requirement, but in reality, they would have been thrilled with an applicant who had two to three years of success in a similar role. Don't keep a great, rule-following job seeker from applying because they think they are unqualified!

Focus on the three to five things that matter most, and save the rest for the interview. The reality is that if they have those three to five things, you will want to speak with them. On the flip side, don't waste people's time (including yours) by not being upfront about something that is a requirement.

Close the deal! Ask them to apply. Let them know what will happen after they do. If you are conducting interviews in the next week, share that with people. Make people feel like this is a real opportunity and a priority for you. Every job seeker has had the experience of completing an application that then disappeared into a black hole. If your job posting smells like that, then people will avoid it. At least, the top performers will.

## MAKE IT EASY TO APPLY

Make sure that your job application is easy to complete from a mobile device. **If your application is not easy, job seekers will abandon it.** And most of the time, companies have no idea. They just figure that not many people have seen the job posting. I remember working with a client who switched over to CareerPlug from another system that was less user-friendly, and they immediately started receiving three times more applicants on the same job postings. The client thought that we were sending the jobs to new places, but we weren't: they were simply getting a much higher percentage of job seekers to complete the application.

Think of these key sections as a series of gates. It starts with the job title and works its way down to next steps. As job seekers review each one, they should be asking themselves, *Is this a good match for me?* If you get the right applicant through each gate, then you will have attracted someone who could end up being a top performer at your company.

Remember, how you position your job in the minds of candidates makes all the difference. Does Enterprise Rent-A-Car highlight the opportunity to wear a suit and stand in a parking lot all day helping people with their rental cars? No. They focus on the opportunity to grow, to run a multi-million-dollar business unit, and to be part of a world-class management training program that produces leaders coveted by almost every other company out there. That is how Enterprise became the #1 recruiter of college graduates in the country.

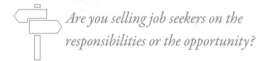 *Are you selling job seekers on the responsibilities or the opportunity?*

Check out our *Job Posting Builder* on **howtohire.com**

# BUILD YOUR LEAD GENERATION SYSTEM

You've written your job posting, and it's up on your careers page. It should be really compelling to the right job seeker. Now, you just need them to start applying, right?

No. There's still lots of work to do. You need to promote your job posting.

Here are three channels that you should use:

1. Your Employees
2. Your Customers & Network
3. Job Boards

These key channels are listed in order of importance. I've talked to many business leaders over the years who skip the first two because they take more work to get results—this is a mistake. Bypassing those channels can cause you to miss out on great candidates that you'll never find on the job boards.

# START WITH EMPLOYEE REFERRALS

Your best customers often come from referrals; the same is true for your best employees. Too many leaders jump right to job boards and ignore their greatest resource. Your employees are a perfect place to start. If someone is a top performer on your team, there is a good chance they hang out with people like them.

The first thing to do here is to let people know that you are hiring. Some of our smaller clients have expressed concerns this might create upheaval at their offices. I advise them to let their teams know that the company is growing and that you are always looking for great people.

Will your current team take notice? Sure, they will! A lot of owners keep people around because they feel they don't have better options, but their perspectives can shift as they find people who would raise the bar for their teams. For current top performers, it's motivating to continually bring on great talent. If someone is upset, this could be a sign that they're a C player, and they may do you a favor by leaving.

The exception to this is when you need to start looking to replace a certain position (usually a managerial or executive role) in which you would never have more than one person. You need to do this discreetly. And in most cases, it's better to part ways with your current employee before you start looking for their replacement.

Motivate your team by creating a referral bonus program. It is one of the best investments that you can make. You only pay it out if you make a hire, and you can make all or part of the bonus contingent upon the new hire still being employed with you months later.

I know a restaurant chain in Austin that spends $500 in referral bonuses for hourly employees. Sometimes they raise it to $1,000 per hire when there is a greater need. They told me that they calculated the value of a hire from a referral, and this bonus provides a great return on investment if the person stays at least six months with them. That's why they pay the bonus to the referring employee six months later, which helps keep that employee around too!

If you are not getting any referrals, then that's a red flag. Start by asking your employees for them. Show gratitude and keep them updated on candidates they've referred. And make a big deal about it when you hire a referred candidate. Recognize the person who gave the referral in front of the company, and remind everyone of the reward they earned.

If that doesn't work, then pull together a group of your most loyal employees and ask them to help you solve this issue. Be ready to listen and make changes—every company needs employee referrals as part of their candidate pool.

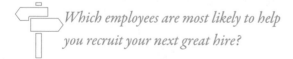 *Which employees are most likely to help you recruit your next great hire?*

# TELL YOUR CUSTOMERS & NETWORK

Your customers are an often-overlooked source of potential candidates and referrals. First, they already do business with you and hopefully love your product or service. Someone who loves to eat at your restaurant or work out at your fitness club has the passion that you want in every one of your employees. Plus, they likely have friends with similar interests—some of whom may be looking for jobs.

Announce that you are hiring with excitement. Make it easy for people to learn more and share it with their friends. Share it through your social media channels and customer newsletters. Share it in your physical location by posting signs in high-visibility areas, like the front door, the counter, or a community message board. I have even seen some clients include this information on receipts!

What if you don't have a business where your customers are potential employees? I still recommend that you tell them about it. Telling people that you are hiring sends the message that you are growing and investing in your business. This shows your confidence and gives them confidence in return. They may have friends or relatives who could be a great match for the position. Plus, this could be great advertising for your business and attract some new customers for you!

You should also let the people in your own network know about your hiring needs. Identify the people who would be most likely to know potential candidates and contact them directly. Let the rest of your network know through social media. Be sure to include a link to the job posting so that people can share it and referred candidates can learn more and apply.

There are certain people in your world who can have a huge impact helping you promote your business. They usually have big networks, and their recommendation carries a lot of weight within them. In the sales world, these people are often referred to as *centers of influence*. Quality beats quantity in these types of relationships.

A client told me about his external center of influence, a high school football coach who introduced him to some of his best employees. He played a major role in the growth and success of his business. Make sure that you know who your centers of influence are and spend a disproportionate amount of your time strengthening those relationships.

Finally, take this message beyond your immediate network and into your community. If you are looking for people with technical backgrounds, build relationships with local trade schools. Offer to speak to their students about starting a career. If you need to hire part-time workers for the summer, connect with schools, churches, and community centers. Or if you know that another employer in your area produces great talent, find a way to connect with people who work there.

Be sure to describe the role you need filled and the type of person you need to fill it. The more details you can provide, the easier it will be for people to make connections in their minds with potential referral candidates. Plus, they will feel much more comfortable contacting someone in their network if they have enough information to know whether your position is a likely match for them.

A word of caution: I have not always had success recruiting from my network. There have been a few times where I hired friends or acquaintances, but I did not stick to my hiring process and evaluation criteria. I put too much weight on the relationship I had with them, and I was too optimistic about them being able to grow into the job (and figure things out along the way). Be sure that you have your team or a trusted advisor hold you accountable to your hiring process (and help you see your blind spots) before you hire a friend.

 *How do you talk with customers about your hiring?*

# WIN ON THE JOB BOARDS

Getting your jobs posted on external job boards is fairly easy. You can either go to each job board and post directly, or you can use an applicant tracking system to distribute them for you.

*Winning* on the job boards is a different story. You enter the competition with thousands of other employers looking for the same people. How will you get noticed, and more importantly, how will you get people to click on your job postings?

First, you need to show up in the right search results. Make sure that you are using a job title and description keywords that the right job seekers will use to find jobs like yours. Also, keep your jobs fresh and up to date. Most job boards will prioritize newer jobs over older ones. Finally, make sure that your job is optimized for mobile applications. Many job boards will show only mobile-friendly postings to people who are searching from their phones—and this is the vast majority of job seekers.

Once you show up in the right search results, you need someone to notice your job posting and click on it. The job title and job description keywords play a huge role here, but so do other factors, such as compensation and employer ratings. Some job boards allow you to post compensation guidance, which shows up in the search results. Job postings with a compensation amount or range listed get significantly more clicks than ones without it. Some job boards now include employer star ratings in search results as well.

Pay attention to this. Even getting a couple of employees to write positive reviews for you can significantly increase the number of people who click on your job.

The best way to optimize your results is to test, measure, and test again. If you have a position for which you recruit on a regular basis, it is worth your time to develop a couple of different job titles and descriptions to evaluate what works best. Measure your results: Which jobs got the most clicks? Which ones converted clicks to applicants at the highest rate? What are your best sources for applicants and hires? This will allow you to refine your process and optimize your results.

Sometimes you will need to generate more results than a standard job posting will provide. Most job boards offer premium or sponsored job posting options, designed to boost the number of people who view and apply to your jobs. This is often necessary to get the results and hires that you need. It's an investment in your growth. I have seen too many leaders sit on an open job posting for months without spending additional money to get the position filled. Sure, there is a cost to driving more applicants. But there is also a cost to having an unfilled position on your team. The cost of the empty seat is almost always greater over time.

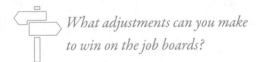

*What adjustments can you make to win on the job boards?*

# HOW MUCH IS A GREAT HIRE WORTH?

Do you know? I bet you have a better idea of what a great customer is worth to you. This helps you determine how much you can spend on marketing efforts to acquire a new one. The same is true for great employees, but leaders usually don't look at it the same way.

Clients have told me that adding a certain type of employee to their teams could increase their revenue by over $100K. These team members would make significantly less money than that, so this would be a tremendous increase in profit for the business.

Despite the huge potential gain, these leaders are often reluctant to invest upfront to attract applicants for these positions. Some will even balk at offering a few hundred dollars as a referral bonus to their current team—even though this position could bring in tens of thousands of dollars of additional profit per year. Meanwhile, they are spending thousands of dollars per month in marketing for new customers.

Even if a great hire may not increase your revenue by six figures, you are probably undervaluing them.

I am all for saving money. I bootstrapped my business and was only able to grow by being fiscally conservative. But there have been times when this mindset hurt me, and I should have invested in our growth. A few years ago, we were really struggling to hire software engineers. We were not getting the results we needed from our traditional channels, and these positions stayed open for many months. The cost of having these openings unfilled was high, and we fell behind. I should have done more (and spent more) to fill them. Don't let this happen to you.

Sometimes there are simply not enough qualified candidates in your market. In this case, you need to get creative, like some of our clients with hard-to-fill positions that they hire for regularly. A plumbing company in a rural market is a great example: there were so few licensed plumbers available that the owner had to attract new people to the profession and train them. The company held information sessions to educate the local workforce on the benefits of a plumbing career and even offered 12-month training programs. It took a lot of work and investment, but each plumber can add $200,000 in annual sales for the business. Plus, the owner has now built a grateful (and loyal) team and an advantage in a market where competitors don't have the staff to take on additional business.

Know how much a great hire is worth to you. If you have a position that could be worth thousands to you, be ready to spend hundreds (or more) to make the hire. Do everything you can to maximize the candidates that you can get for free, but don't stop there if you have not gotten what you need. It will cost you more in the long run.

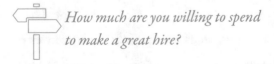 *How much are you willing to spend to make a great hire?*

Check out our *Value/Cost Per Hire Calculator* on **howtohire.com**

# MAKE IT EASY TO APPLY!

You have done a great job getting job seekers to click on your job posting to learn more—but it won't matter if they don't apply.

There was a time when applicants, particularly hourly workers, were willing to spend 30 minutes on a job application. This was the standard. It was simply the way things were done.

Well, not anymore.

Most job seekers use their mobile devices to search and apply for jobs. And they are no longer willing to complete long applications upfront. There are too many alternatives from employers offering applications that can be completed in minutes (or less) from any device. If you mandate a long application process, you will only be left with a fraction of your potential applicants. And they probably won't be top performers.

Would you ever make a prospective customer fill out a long application upfront? If you run a business that relies on getting sales leads from the internet, imagine what would happen to your lead volume if prospects had to complete a form that took 30 minutes. What if that application asked for sensitive information like your Social Security Number? You would have no leads!

You may be thinking: What about all of the information that needs to be collected as part of the application process? You can still capture all of that—just do it as a second step in the process. Use the first step to capture the lead and any essentials you need to measure initial qualifications. Then use the second step to capture any additional required information that is not critical to the first evaluation.

Almost all job seekers have spent time completing a detailed resume to include in the application. Don't make them repeat this work by asking them to complete a form documenting their last three employers. Sure, there may be a few applicants who do not have a resume, but you should not put every applicant through this because of these exceptions. Or maybe you don't even need a resume upfront for certain jobs.

Never ask applicants for sensitive information like their Social Security Number or date of birth upfront. Put yourself in their shoes. You probably would not want to provide this to someone you don't know. Your applicants feel the same way.

Wait until the second step for assessments and forms that someone may not be prepared to complete at that moment. Applicants may not have the time or the right information to complete all of that initially.

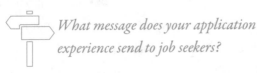 *What message does your application experience send to job seekers?*

---

Check out our *Grade Your Application Experience* exercise on **howtohire.com**

---

Great leads are like French fries: they are at their best when they are fresh and hot!

You don't let your sales team sit on great leads—even waiting an hour can be too long. So, why are you okay with waiting a week to follow up with a great candidate? Would you ever expect a potential customer to wait that long? They are excited to learn more about your business and ready to talk. But if you wait too long, they are going to pursue other options. And just like sales prospects, great candidates always have other options.

How fast do you need to be? I know companies that have escalation alerts sent out if sales leads are not contacted within five minutes. That may be extreme for recruiting, but some owners tell me that prospects for certain positions will be gone and off the market if they cannot reach them in 48 hours. Think about what the standard should be for you and your team, and hold everyone accountable to sticking to it.

Speed gets you ahead of your competition, but persistence is often what gets you the sale. If you had a great sales lead come in, how would you react if your team simply sent them an email and then gave up? This is how most people recruit.

Some people say that recruiting is different: these people want a job that you have, so if they don't respond to your email, they must be unreliable. This mindset is out of touch with reality. The competition for talent is fierce, and it has never been easier for people to apply to jobs. Great candidates have lots of options. You need to show that you are genuinely interested in recruiting them for your opportunity. Sometimes this takes more than an email. Follow up with a text or pick up the phone and give them a call.

Don't let a great candidate lead slip through the cracks because you were not fast or persistent enough.

 *What changes can you make to get back to candidates faster?*

# ALWAYS BE RECRUITING

When you recruit like you sell, you never stop recruiting. You're always out there, looking for the next prospect.

Think about when you meet someone new—I bet you spend a minute wondering whether they would be a good customer for you. I do this all the time. This can be annoying to my wife, but sometimes she likes to play along or even initiate it!

This is called opportunity awareness. Every successful entrepreneur has it.

Now, you just need to channel it toward your most important sale—your next hire. I call this your *talent radar*.

You never know where you are going to find high-quality people. It could be the sales rep at the wireless store who helped you upgrade your phone. Or a bartender at a restaurant who made you feel like you were his only customer. It could even be your friend's son or daughter who is home from college for the summer. You don't know when the right person will show up, so you need to keep your talent radar activated at all times.

This talent radar helped me make one of my best all-time hires: Chris, our sales leader. At the time, he was working for a client of ours. We had lunch one day when he was in Austin, and he let me know that he was planning to leave his current employer because he needed to relocate to Texas to be closer to family. He asked me if I knew anyone who was hiring. The crazy part of this story was that it was my wife's talent radar that went off - not mine! I came home and told her that Chris was looking for a job in Texas, and she reminded me that he could be perfect for the sales leader opening that I had. It did not occur to me at first because, in my mind, I needed someone who had experience selling software. But the more I thought about it, the more it made perfect sense to speak with Chris about it. While he hadn't sold software, he knew our target client very well (he was that person). Plus, he had strong sales experience in a different industry as well as deep knowledge of our software. And that turned out to be exactly what we needed.

The key is to be ready to recruit at any moment. Some of our clients have created recruiting-specific business cards for this purpose. They hand them out when they meet people who impress them.

This sounds like extra work. And it is. But it's nothing like the extra work you will have when you end up shorthanded and struggling as a result. When you are reactive and desperate while hiring, you let your guard down and compromise your standards. You want relief and you want it now! Don't let that happen to you.

The best results in recruiting come from having a handful of interested and highly qualified people ready to come work for you as soon as you have an opening. You get there by having a great opportunity and being a great place to work—and by building your pipeline.

Think about the key roles at your company. Do you have at least two or three people that you could call if you had an unexpected opening? This is your pipeline. You develop it by always having a recruiting mindset and by staying in touch with people. It does not have to be all of the time—just send them a note once in a while. Ask how they are doing. Share an interesting article with them. Show them that you are still interested.

You never know what opportunities may arise when you are always recruiting. You may meet someone who is such a potential asset to your company that you decide to make a hire even though you don't have an opening. What if you had the option to hire someone with the potential to help you grow your business significantly? That will happen if you are always recruiting and looking for opportunities in the same way that you sell.

*Who would you call today if you found out that a key employee was leaving?*

# SCHEDULE THE INTERVIEW!

INTERVIEWS, NOT APPLICANTS

BEAT THE SLOG

HOW TO READ A RESUME

PRESCREEN FIRST

MAKE A DECISION!

SCHEDULE LIKE A PRO

# INTERVIEWS, NOT APPLICANTS

Sometimes clients come to us saying they have an applicant problem. They think that increasing the number of qualified applicants they get will solve the problem. Having more qualified applicants coming in always helps, but it's often not the root of the issue.

Here's the reality: Most companies stink at converting their applicants to interviews.

When I take a look at a client's applicant pool, I usually see some qualified candidates there. But then I see that it took the client over a week to contact them about next steps. And often that came in the form of a generic email.

They think they have an applicant problem. But they really have an interview problem. An interview conversion problem to be more precise.

Let's say that you need to interview three candidates to make the right hire. You could get there by receiving five qualified applicants and converting 60% of them to interviews. Or you could find a way to get 20 qualified applicants and convert 15% of them to interviews.

These two scenarios produced the same outcome (three interviews), but one got there much more efficiently. And you may not have the luxury of being able to attract 20 qualified applicants for your position—at least not without having to spend a bunch of money to advertise it.

Here's the good news: There's a straightforward way to improve your interview conversion rate. It just takes a little more planning and a lot more urgency.

*Do you have an applicant problem or an interview problem?*

# BEAT THE SLOG

This is often the most frustrating part of the process for everyone. Applicants have applied for jobs, but they have not heard from you. You have received their applications, but they won't respond to you. And you are wondering who all of these unqualified people are who keep applying and wasting your time!

Applicants sometimes refer to this phase as *the black hole* because they apply to jobs and never receive responses from the companies. I like to call it *the slog*.

This period can be just as stressful for you as it is for applicants. If you did a good job of marketing your open position, then you may be overwhelmed by all of the applications you have received. You probably didn't plan for this and are now trying to fit hiring into your already busy workday. After all, you are short-staffed and may be temporarily doing the job of the person you are trying to hire. I have been there, and just thinking about those times stresses me out.

All you can see is an inbox flooded with resumes, and many of them look horrible to you. It's kind of like coming back from vacation to an inbox filled with hundreds of unread emails—except you didn't get to go on vacation! The worst part is that there are high-quality candidates in there, and you are losing them. Every minute you wait, they are talking to other employers and taking other jobs.

You can escape the slog, but you need a system. And you need to commit time to stick to it.

Reviewing applicants is a lot like managing your email. People who don't have a good system get stressed out by it. But the same things that help you become more productive with your email will help you manage your applicants more effectively:

**Create a daily routine for reviewing applicants.** It really needs to happen at least once a day. I would recommend that you do it two to three times a day in the first couple of weeks after you post the job since that is when you will receive the most applicants. Put this time on your calendar and stick to it. Try to make it the same time(s) each day.

**Create time blocks for interviews.** When you are in the zone processing your emails, it's not the time to get deep into working on one specific email. David Allen from *Getting Things Done* suggests that if something takes two minutes or less to do, then you should do it immediately. Otherwise, you should make time to do it later. You should be able to review an application and take the next step in two minutes or less, so that should be your focus while you are processing applications. Don't try to start interviewing people on the spot. You should create separate time blocks for interviewing and invite candidates to speak with you at these times.

There are exceptions to this rule. Sometimes a certain email comes in and makes you drop everything to address it. You may get an exceptional applicant that makes you do the same thing. In this case, pick up the phone and call them (or send them a text).

**Take action and keep things clean.** You need to be decisive at this stage. Move the applicant to the next step or reject them. Some people get paralyzed here. They don't want to commit to bringing them in for an interview or rejecting them. They want to see who else comes in. They think: "What if this is the best candidate that I'll get?" This kind of thinking will stall your process and clog your inbox (and thinking). Make a decision and move them away from other applicants who need to be reviewed.

**Accept that you will receive some "unwanted emails."** Think of unqualified applicants the same way you think about the unwanted email that you receive. It can be frustrating, but you need to accept this as an unavoidable part of the hiring process. Some applicants may look unqualified on the surface but could be hidden gems. Others are just straight-up unqualified and leave you wondering why they even bothered to apply. Just like those kinds of emails, remove them and move on.

I have clients who have gotten so upset by these applicants that it messed up their mindsets. When I reviewed the applicants who actually had applied, there were some qualified candidates in there that they had not even noticed. Email systems like Gmail have developed ways to identify unwanted emails. You need to do the same thing with your applicants, whether through the use of an applicant tracking system or some other strategy you develop.

The slog is real, but you can beat it. When things get chaotic, your best bet is to get organized. I always tell my team that ten minutes spent getting organized usually saves me an hour of work. Developing a system and sticking to it will do the same for you.

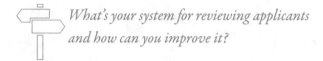

*What's your system for reviewing applicants and how can you improve it?*

# HOW TO READ A RESUME

Resumes are the universal currency for job applications: they are not perfect, but they are still important. The rise of online applications has made the resume more common, even for positions like fast food workers and janitors. You may not want to require a resume for certain roles, but you will be surprised by how many candidates have them.

Here is what goes through my mind when I look at a resume. (It may vary some by position, but not much.)

## WHERE ARE THEY LOCATED?

I always look to see if the candidate lives in the area. If you don't recognize the address, then type the ZIP/postal code into an online search. If you get a qualified candidate who does not live nearby, don't rule them out just yet. It may be worth a conversation (or at least an email/text) to see if they plan to relocate to your area.

## WHAT HAVE THEY ACCOMPLISHED?

Take a look at the candidate's track record as an employee. Do they have relevant work experience? I like to look deeper than the company name and job title: Look at how the candidate describes their responsibilities and their impact. This tells you a lot about someone and what they value. I would be more impressed by someone who worked in an unrelated job but clearly took ownership in the work and made a big impact than someone who worked in the right type of job but didn't have much to say about what they accomplished. You will need to flesh this out more in the interviews, but first impressions matter.

Don't forget that someone's potential is often worth much more than their experience. Every star employee had to start somewhere. Someone gave them a shot before they had any relevant experience. On the flip side, just because someone has had a job in your field does not mean that they are the one that you want to hire. Think of the people who were C players for you. Now they have your company name and job title on their resume. You may be looking at someone else's C players!

## ARE THEY RELIABLE?

Take a look at the story that the resume tells you: Do you see a rising star or an inconsistent job hopper? Past behavior is usually a good predictor of the future. If someone has not stayed in a job for more than six months in the past five years, what makes you think that they are going to change that behavior for you? Some employers will set strict rules about this when screening, such as no more than three jobs in the past five years. It's not always that easy, especially for candidates who are earlier in their careers. I don't count job-hopping against a college student the same way I would against a professional in the workforce—but I do give extra credit to the college student who works at the same job throughout school.

## WHAT KIND OF EDUCATION
## DO THEY HAVE?

The education section of a resume is important to different employers for different reasons. If you are hiring for a professional role, the right degree is a minimum. This also applies to skilled trades like plumbing or cosmetology. Look to see if they list the relevant licenses. This section may also give you a clue into someone's availability. If you are hiring for a part-time position, it's good to know that someone goes to school nearby and with many of your other employees. If the person graduated last fall, you may be wondering why this person is applying for a part-time position. Along the same lines, what if a person applies for a full-time position while they are still in school? Are they applying to start work once they graduate, or perhaps only going to school part-time? These are things you will want to clarify during an initial conversation (or by simply asking them over text or email before you extend an interview invitation).

## WHAT SKILLS DO THEY POSSESS?

The skills section can be informative on a couple of levels. First, you may learn that the candidate has certain skills that will be valuable to the position (and may even be required). This may be the ability to speak Spanish or the ability to write software code in a certain programming language. The skills that a candidate highlights also show areas of interest. If a candidate lists that they can type 80 words per minute, it makes me think that they are interested in clerical work. If they list a proficiency with a sales tracking software, then I know they have worked in sales and probably want to continue working in that field.

## WHAT DO THEY DO OUTSIDE OF WORK?

The extracurriculars section is highly underrated. It's not a requirement to have one, but I often learn more about a person from this area of the resume than any other. What kinds of activities does this person participate in outside of work? Are they simply a participant, or are they a leader? Think about successful hires you have made in the past and look for trends. At CareerPlug, we have done well with people who devote significant time to volunteering, since giving back is an important part of our culture. Some organizations do really well hiring people who have been athletes; we have had a lot of success with candidates who come from musical and theatrical backgrounds. I have found these candidates to be highly detail-oriented and disciplined. We also tend to attract a lot of people who value travel. This can be an indicator of curiosity and open-mindedness, both of which are common traits of our best employees and tied to our core value of *Keep Growing*. This is also great material to use in interviews to connect with candidates and get them to be more open.

## WHAT IMPRESSION DOES THIS CANDIDATE GIVE YOU?

Consider the tone, language, and grammar they used. Look for spelling and grammar mistakes. These may give you clues about someone's education level as well as their attention to detail. Does the resume match the job? The resume that a potential teacher creates may look quite different than someone applying to work at a bank. One of my best hires had a resume with a unique layout that highlighted her superpowers. It showed me right away that she was not afraid to take an unconventional path—something that I value.

## IS THERE A COVER LETTER?

We encourage our clients to have a place for applicants to include cover letters in an application. I don't like to make it a requirement because I want to see if they submit one themselves. For entry-level or blue-collar roles, a cover letter is not expected but is always appreciated. For more senior roles, I expect to see one. The cover letter itself is a valuable extension of the resume. It gives you a sense of someone's motivation and goals. The qualifications and accomplishments that they highlight show what they value in themselves. Plus, you get to see their written communication skills.

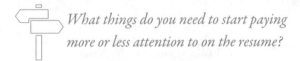

*What things do you need to start paying more or less attention to on the resume?*

# PRESCREEN FIRST

Resumes can tell you a lot of things, including someone's job history and education, but they do not provide the full picture that you need to assess a candidate—including some of the most important facets. This is particularly true for entry-level roles when you are hiring someone more for their potential than for their track record.

This is why we include basic qualifying questions (we call them *prescreen questions*) as part of our application. Prescreen questions allow you to identify highly qualified applicants as well as unqualified ones right away. And they may be the biggest time saver in the entire hiring process. I always look at the prescreen responses before I review a resume.

Think about the most important criteria for the position and develop prescreen questions for them. What are the first few things you would want to know about this person? These could be items that should be on their resume, such as their level of experience. But the best kind of questions ask about things that you otherwise would not learn until the interview, such as someone's work availability.

Here are some common types of prescreen questions:

**Experience:** *How many years of sales experience do you have?*

**Certification:** *What type of personal training certification do you have?*

**Language:** *How well do you speak Spanish?*

**Availability:** *Are you able to work nights and weekends?*

**Driving:** *Do you have a valid driver's license?*

You will get the most value from prescreen questions by developing a scoring system for applicants based on their responses. This will allow you to identify top prospects and disqualify certain applicants. Focus on questions with a fixed set of answer options (versus open-ended response fields), so that you can assign a score value to each one. (We use CareerPlug's applicant tracking system to do this.)

Some employers also like to add an open-ended question to see how someone thinks. One of our favorites is "What makes you unique?" We have learned a lot about applicants by the way they answer this. Some have been serious and listed specific accomplishments. Others have been playful and shared a funny story about themselves. One of our clients, a popular Texas taco chain, asks "What's your favorite taco and why?" They wanted to focus on hiring people who already love to eat at their restaurant, and this is their way of doing it.

We recommend using three to five prescreen questions and no more than one open-ended question. If you use more than that, you start to deter job seekers from applying, especially from their phones. Plus, having a laundry list of prescreen questions takes your focus away from the handful of things that are most important. You don't need to know everything about applicants at this stage—just enough to make a decision on whether to move them to the next step. There will be plenty of time to ask them more questions during the interview process.

When you receive applications with a prescreen score, it makes it easier to focus on your top candidates. Think about how much more effective you will be at focusing on your top five candidates versus all twenty-five applicants; this might be the difference between connecting with the right person for an interview and letting them slip through the cracks.

 *What are the top three things that you want to know about an applicant that you cannot find on their resume?*

# MAKE A DECISION!

You need to make a decision—and fast! Your goal here is to convert qualified applicants into interviews. That is the only way that you are going to make hires!

Think about this as a fork in the road. Do you want to move this person into the hiring process or do you want to dismiss them? Don't postpone this decision and leave people in a middle ground. Move them to the next step or reject them. If you don't act quickly, qualified applicants are going to look somewhere else. Remember, you are not giving them an offer at this point, you're just committing to move them forward to the next step. This may be as simple as asking them to complete an assessment or have a quick phone call. If there is something on the resume that is hanging you up—such as their location—send them a quick text or email and ask them about it.

Don't ignore the unqualified applicants. The best thing you can do for someone who is not a good fit is send them a quick and encouraging rejection email. Thank them for applying and let them know that you have decided to move forward with another candidate—and wish them luck in their job search! You should aim to create a great experience for each candidate. Don't forget, they may be current (or potential) customers of yours. They also may be a great fit for a role with you after getting some experience somewhere else.

This takes a little extra work, but it is worth it. And if you use an applicant tracking system, you can streamline (or even automate) this process.

How you treat all candidates says a lot about your company and culture. We have received referrals from candidates who did not get hired by us simply because they were impressed by our follow-up.

 *What is keeping you from acting faster on applicants?*

# SCHEDULE LIKE A PRO

You cannot have a successful interview unless you get it scheduled. Don't take this for granted. In a competitive job market, qualified applicants do not last long (just like good sales leads). Here's how the best recruiters beat the competition and convert qualified applicants into interviews:

## PERSONALIZE IT

Show the candidate that you are excited to speak with them, and try to make the message as personalized as possible. One little note about their most recent job or where they went to school can go a long way in creating a connection (and getting an enthusiastic response from them).

You can also personalize it by making it stand out from the other messages they receive. Every applicant who applies for a position at CareerPlug gets to watch a video from Natalie, our People leader, introducing herself and our company. She spends a minute talking about our hiring process and what to expect. Candidates have told us that they love this! It's a little thing, but it goes a long way to create a connection with candidates.

## SEND A TEXT

Don't rely on email to get the job done. Most people don't check their email regularly, and it will end up in a pile with a bunch of unimportant emails. Text messaging has become the most effective channel for candidate communication, particularly for entry-level and hourly roles. If you are looking for a quick response, nothing beats a text message. Don't want to text from your personal cell phone? You can use an applicant tracking system to send texts directly to candidates.

Texting candidates is not appropriate for all roles and situations. It's important to consider your audience and the type of message that you need to communicate. Sometimes it makes more sense to email or call a candidate.

## MAKE IT EASY

If you know that you want to interview someone, make it as easy as possible to schedule it. The best recruiters share their availability with candidates upfront and allow them to book the time that works best for them (without any of the typical back and forth coordination). This could be as simple as including some time slots in your message or using scheduling software to display your availability and book interviews.

## BE FIRST

Be decisive and take action quickly. Some clients say that the shelf life of a good applicant in their field is 48 hours—meaning if you have not spoken with them by that time, you probably never will. Many job seekers will take the first job they are offered, so you really don't have time to wait—even if your job opportunity would be perfect for them.

Al Ries and Jack Trout put it best in *The 22 Immutable Laws of Marketing*: "It's better to be first than it is to be better."

If you don't think that you can get back to candidates quickly enough, consider automating the initial contact. We built a feature called Autopilot in CareerPlug to help clients who were in this situation. While an automated text/email message won't give you the same personalized touch, it could be the difference between you scheduling an interview (or not).

 *How much energy are you putting into converting applicants into interviews?*

# INTERVIEW FOR THE BIG THREE

ONLY THREE THINGS MATTER

CAN THEY DO IT?

EVALUATE FOR ABILITY

WILL THEY DO IT?

EVALUATE FOR MOTIVATION

WILL OTHERS DO IT WITH THEM?

EVALUATE FOR CULTURE FIT

INTERVIEW LIKE A PRO

KEEP IT OBJECTIVE

KEEP YOUR SCORECARD SIMPLE

YOU'RE BEING INTERVIEWED TOO

# ONLY THREE THINGS MATTER

When I think about the hiring process, only three things matter when evaluating a candidate:

1. Can they do it? (Ability)
2. Will they do it? (Motivation)
3. Will others do it with them? (Culture fit)

That's it.

*Note: This chapter includes a description of the different ways you can evaluate candidates for ability, motivation and culture fit. Chapter 7 will cover how to choose the right evaluation steps for your company/job and organize them into your hiring process.*

# CAN THEY DO IT?

The first and most basic question in hiring—yet companies and hiring managers are often fooled by this step for a few key reasons. First, they do not understand (and clearly document) the talents/skills that are most important for success in the role. Second, they fail to differentiate between what a candidate must already possess versus what can be developed on the job. And last, they don't have a system to consistently evaluate talents/skills during the hiring process. Suddenly, this question isn't so easy to answer.

Do not confuse "Can they do it?" with "Have they done it?" When you evaluate someone on a certain talent or skill, ask yourself, "Am I requiring this experience because it's essential from day one? Or am I requiring this because I don't want to go through the trouble of training them or feel like I'm making a risky hire?" If it's the latter, think carefully about this decision. You could be needlessly eliminating a huge segment of the talent pool.

Remember that "Can they do it?" is a different question than "Have they done it?"

It seems like it would be great if they have done it already. Sounds like a sure thing. It isn't.

Sure, lots of people may have done it already. But how many of them are A Players? Many A Players have been there and done that, and now they are ready to move up. B Players often stay in the same job for the long run—they are not always looking. C Players quit or get fired from jobs more often. And a lot of them are applying to your job. Just because they've done it before doesn't mean that they can do it well for you.

Sometimes hiring proven talent isn't even an option. If you're hiring for an entry-level role, you have to hire for potential. These positions, by definition, are starting points in someone's career.

You cannot expect to attract experienced applicants—at least not the good ones—by offering entry-level compensation. If you are not willing to pay for experience, then you have to be willing to hire for potential and develop them yourself. Many employers prefer this approach since it allows them to train new hires in their way of doing things without having to break bad habits learned at other companies in the same industry.

There are certain situations where it makes sense to pay up for proven talent: 1) When you hire for a new position where you don't have subject matter expertise to train someone yourselves, and 2) When the value of experience far outweighs the additional cost for it.

There are plenty of potential pitfalls in hiring for potential. And you will certainly experience them. You will have someone leave after you invested time to train them but before they ever produce for you.

But I know one thing for sure: there is nothing more satisfying than hiring someone for their potential and seeing them develop into an A Player under your guidance.

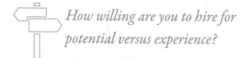

*How willing are you to hire for potential versus experience?*

# EVALUATE FOR ABILITY

You won't be able to do this until you identify the three to five talents or skills that are critical to success in the role. This is particularly important for evaluating a candidate's ability. You should document all of this on your Ideal Candidate Profile.

Don't make the mistake of using a long list of requirements.

I was reminded of this recently while hiring for a new director at CareerPlug. I had a list of about ten talents/skills that I wanted to see in this person. When I sat down with my leadership team to discuss the role and our top prospects, we had a healthy debate over which criteria mattered most. I recognized my own mistake here—focusing on ten things was too much—so I asked each leader to rank their top five criteria from the current list. We shared our thoughts as a team and decided on a list of the five most important talents/skills. When we interviewed the right person, it was crystal clear to everyone on the leadership team that we had found our next director.

Once you have identified these talents/skills, you need to determine how you will know whether a candidate possesses them. You need to look at who the candidate is today and where they have been. Here are the evaluation methods that we use.

## PERSONALITY ASSESSMENTS

These help you understand whether a candidate has the natural talents to succeed in a position. For example, a sales position typically requires someone who is outgoing, assertive, and resilient. A personality assessment can help you measure these traits in a candidate and evaluate their potential. This is particularly valuable if the candidate has never held this type of role. People have the ability to adjust their personality and succeed in a role that is not naturally suited to them, but this becomes more challenging over time. That being said, I would put less weight on someone's personality assessment if they already have a successful track record working in a similar position.

It is important to identify the personality traits that are important to success in the role and focus on those. Some employers make the mistake of testing for a large inventory of personality traits and lose focus of what is truly important. Focus on quality over quantity.

## COGNITIVE ASSESSMENTS

These help you understand whether a candidate has the intellectual capabilities to be successful in a position. The tests can evaluate math and verbal skills, critical thinking, and attention to detail. It is well-established that people with higher cognitive abilities are usually higher performers at work. The challenge that some employers face is understanding what type of level of cognitive ability is appropriate for a certain role. For example, the cognitive abilities necessary for an engineer are quite different from those required of a customer support representative. Make sure that you have the appropriate assessment for the position, and then give the assessment to current employees who are in that role. This will help you create benchmarks for acceptable scores.

## SPECIFIC INTERVIEW QUESTIONS

You can learn a lot about someone's ability by examining their overall experience, but it usually makes sense to dig deeper to evaluate specific talents and skills. You should have a set of interview questions tied to each talent or skill that you identified as being critical for the role. It is best to ask open-ended questions. Some of these questions will be experience-based: "Tell me about a time when you had to take a stand for something," for example, may be a question used to check for assertiveness. Other questions may look for a candidate's knowledge or philosophy. "How do you define exceptional customer service?" could be an appropriate question for service orientation. Aim for two to three questions for each talent or skill you evaluate. If you are not satisfied with the response, you can always dig deeper by asking follow-up questions, like "Can you tell me more?" or "What's another example of this?"

## JOB SIMULATION

This is the interview where the candidate gets to work to show you their ability. The job simulation allows you to give candidates a preview of the work related to the job, evaluate their ability in doing the work, and observe how they react to feedback you provide on their performance.

The nature of this interview varies by role. For our support representatives, we do a support call simulation and also ask them to respond to a support email. For account executives, we ask them to conduct a sales presentation. Each simulation is followed by feedback provided by a manager (and in some cases, a peer).

The results of this technique have shown me that there is no substitute for seeing how candidates actually work. There have been some candidates who did just okay in traditional interviews, but they shined in this stage. We've also had candidates who said all of the right things in previous interviews but then fell flat with the job simulation.

Be sure to give some constructive feedback on areas that they can improve after the simulation. In certain situations, we will give a candidate another shot at the simulation to see whether they could adjust based on the feedback they were given. We have also had candidates get quite defensive when they receive feedback, raising important red flags for the hiring manager.

Sometimes we will ask candidates to complete a homework assignment. Often the homework is related to the job simulation interview (working on a software code challenge or preparing a sales presentation), but it could also be something different, such as compiling some writing samples from previous jobs or submitting a new writing sample.

In addition to evaluating their homework (ability), this step is designed to see whether they will actually complete the homework (motivation). There have been plenty of candidates who disappeared after we asked them to do some homework. Besides reviewing the quality of the work delivered, you should observe how they interact with you throughout the process. What questions did they ask you about the homework upfront? Did they make a commitment to you to deliver it by a certain date? Did they hit that deadline? These are clues into how they will work with you in the future.

While having someone deliver the completed assignment to you the next day can show their eagerness, that's not the most important thing to me. Most top performers are busy people with commitments to their current jobs and families. I'd rather have someone tell me upfront that they need a week to complete it and then deliver quality work on time.

Regardless of the steps you take, you should not hire someone until you are confident in their ability to succeed in the role. Take the time to understand the skills and talents that are critical for success, and then develop specific plans to evaluate them. If you don't do this, then you are relying on your gut. That's not the worst thing. Your instincts will certainly help you. But what happens when you need others to do the interviewing and hiring for you?

You won't be able to grow.

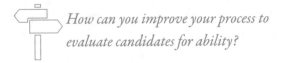

*How can you improve your process to evaluate candidates for ability?*

# WILL THEY DO IT?

"Can they do it?" does not mean much if they are not *willing* to do it. Most people can suck it up and do just about anything for the short term. People have a way of convincing themselves that they can make it work. But one day, they just won't be able to make it work anymore.

Turnover (and all of the work that comes with it) is a productivity killer. It can be a business killer too. You need people who are going to be with you for the long haul, and you need to invest in them and make them integral parts of your team. To achieve this, you need to hire people who are motivated to succeed with you.

I continue to be amazed at what people can accomplish with the right motivation. Clients have told me stories about candidates who were previously landscapers or delivery drivers and are now their best salespeople. Usually, there's another part of the story—a young man who immigrated from another country and wants to send money home to his family; a single mother who wants to provide a better life for her children; a recent college graduate who wants to pay off student loans and then start a business.

On the flip side, I have seen several people with far more natural talent absolutely squander it. Ability is worthless unless you have the drive to put it to work.

If you find someone with the right motivation, give them an opportunity and watch how hard they will work for you (and themselves).

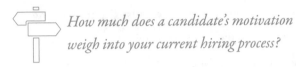

*How much does a candidate's motivation weigh into your current hiring process?*

# EVALUATE FOR MOTIVATION

Everyone is motivated by something. It's your job to evaluate whether a candidate's motivation aligns with what you need at your company.

The best way to evaluate a candidate's motivation is to look at where they have been and where they are headed. You can learn a lot by listening to someone's life story and then asking them about their goals. We use the Lifeline Interview for this purpose. With high performers, the motivation usually comes through loud and clear. If it doesn't, then you need to think twice before making the hire.

## THE LIFELINE INTERVIEW

This interview is designed to give you a deeper understanding of where someone has been and where they are headed.

The first part is a walk-through of a candidate's past. You will be amazed by how much better you understand a person once you've seen the path they have taken to get where they are. We start by asking them to tell us about where they are from and anything about their upbringing that influenced who they have become. This should focus the conversation on a handful of significant events or people.

Next, we ask them about their education. If they went to college, we'll focus there. If not, we talk about their time in high school.

We ask about the highs and lows they experienced through this period, as well as what they learned. Then we ask how they transitioned to the next part of their life.

After that, we cover a candidate's employment history in chronological order. We usually limit this to their three most recent jobs.

For each job, we typically ask candidates:

- Tell us about the company and your position/responsibilities.
- What attracted you to this job?
- Tell us about your experience working there. What did you like/not like about it?
- Tell us about your manager. What would they say are your strengths and weaknesses?
- What were your highs/lows?
- What were your dates of employment at this job? (Compare against what's listed on their resume.)
- Why did you leave? (Make sure you know whether the candidate resigned or was let go due to a layoff or termination.)
- What did you learn?

You can learn a lot by listening to someone's story. Look for insights and patterns. Why did they leave their last job? How do they talk about their past? Are they taking responsibility for what has happened in their lives, or are they victims?

The second part of the Lifeline Interview asks a candidate to envision their future. We ask them to think ahead three years from now and describe what their best life looks like in as much detail as possible. We encourage them to talk about their career as well as what they are comfortable sharing from their personal life, which may include things like family, health, community, travel, or a hobby.

Next, we ask them to talk to us about their plan to achieve this vision. Check to see whether they know how to get there. Ask if they have set any specific goals.

Then, we ask them why accomplishing these things is important to them. We also ask how it will make them feel. This is where you get into people's deep-down motivation and start to understand what drives them.

Finally, and most importantly, we ask the candidate: "Based on what you know about this career opportunity, can you see yourself accomplishing all of this while working here?"

This is a critical question that really asks whether this job is going to allow the candidate to accomplish their personal goals. If there is true alignment, this should be an exciting feeling for the candidate. You have shown them a path to get what they want out of life. Plus, you have shown them that you care about that. If you sense any hesitation, ask some clarifying questions and encourage the candidate to do the same. This often helps surface specific questions regarding growth trajectory, work/life balance, or compensation. It's better to address these topics now so that everything is clear prior to you making an offer.

This is easily the most positive and motivating interview in the hiring process. Candidates consistently tell us how refreshing our process is, and a lot of that has to do with this interview.

As a manager, you have just been given pure gold. You now know what motivates this person and you can use that to more effectively lead them. Imagine how good everyone will feel if you review this three years later and everything has come true! Be sure to capture the notes from this interview so that they can be reviewed and revised in the future.

The Lifeline Interview is a cornerstone of our evaluation process. While we categorize it as a motivation interview, it hits on all of the Big Three criteria: ability, motivation, and culture fit. In addition to understanding how they got here and where they are headed, it gives you a view of their experience and track record (ability) and what they value (culture fit).

We conduct the Lifeline Interview as a second-round interview and allow 60 minutes to complete it.

 *How clear are you on a candidate's goals before you hire them?*

---

Check out our *Lifeline Interview Guide* on **howtohire.com**

---

# WILL OTHERS DO IT WITH THEM?

Culture fit is non-negotiable for companies that want to build truly great teams. Some companies fall into the trap of making culture fit exceptions for high performers. This is a direct route to a toxic culture.

Measuring culture fit can be tricky. One mistake I often see is defining culture fit as "Who looks like us?" Going down this path often leads to a lack of diversity on your team and a failure to build a healthy, inclusive company culture.

Culture fit should start with your company's core values. People work better together when there are shared values between them. Make sure your interviews incorporate questions around your core values.

Here's the great news: The right candidates will become that much more attracted to you if they can see that the company has similar values to them. We make our core values visible during our hiring process. Top candidates frequently call out our values-driven approach to hiring as a key factor in choosing to apply and ultimately work with us.

You should also understand a candidate's work preferences. Does their work style match up with yours? Do your people move fast and worry about the details later? Then think twice about hiring someone from a slow, bureaucratic company. Do you have an active, open office environment? Might not want to hire that person who needs a quiet space to get anything done. Casual dress policy at work? The professional with a closet full of corporate power suits may feel totally lost.

Culture fit may be the toughest to evaluate out of the three. Make sure to include your team in the interview process. They may be much more likely to pick up on certain things than you will. Plus, they will be the ones who need to work with this person each day. Give them a voice in the process. Remember to be authentic with your culture and give a realistic view of your company. Let candidates evaluate if they are the right culture fit at the same time that you're evaluating them.

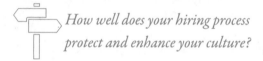

*How well does your hiring process protect and enhance your culture?*

# EVALUATE FOR CULTURE FIT

You and your team should be evaluating the candidate for culture fit throughout the interview process. Here are some ways that you can do this.

## INTERVIEW QUESTIONS

Our interview scorecards include a section to evaluate candidates for alignment with our core values. Usually, we are able to pick up on these things throughout the interview. For example, one of our values is *Keep Growing*. At the end of the interview, the interviewers need to assess whether this value seemed important to the candidate. Did the candidate show that they were committed to improving themselves? For the right candidates, these values should shine through during the interview. If they don't, you should ask yourself why.

In some cases, we use specific interview questions. Like the questions focused on a specific talent or skill, these usually ask a candidate to either share a relevant experience or a viewpoint related to a specific core value. Here are a couple that we use: "Tell us about a time you had to communicate something difficult to a peer or manager" demonstrates their ability to *Speak Up, Step Up*, and "How do you handle situations when you need to work closely with someone who operates differently than you?" helps us evaluate a candidate on their ability to *Work Together, Win Together*.

## JOB SHADOW

Job shadowing makes sense when you are hiring entry-level candidates who have never done a job like this previously. This could involve sitting with the support team and listening to calls or even doing a field ride with a sales rep or technician to observe their daily routine. It's important to pair the candidate with a senior person in that role. Your candidates will get a hands-on job preview, and your trusted employee will get to evaluate how candidates conduct themselves and the types of questions they ask along the way.

## PEER LUNCH

This is a great way to measure culture fit and get your team involved in the process. It's simple: have your team take the candidate to lunch without you. The last part (without you) is important because it gives everyone a chance to get to know each other in a more casual setting. Candidates will often feel more comfortable asking certain questions or speaking candidly when the boss is not around.

Sometimes candidates will show their true colors at lunch. I can think of at least one candidate who got very casual with our team and started making inappropriate comments at lunch. Other times were not as jarring, but team members have reported back that they felt it would be hard to work with certain candidates. This step has definitely saved us from some bad hires.

No matter how you do it, get your team involved in the hiring process. This shows them that you care about their opinions; plus it provides different perspectives which will highlight things you may have overlooked. Most importantly, it gives your team a vested interest in making this hire a success. If the team goes to bat for a candidate, you can hold them accountable for doing everything they can to help your new hire succeed.

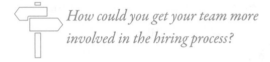

*How could you get your team more involved in the hiring process?*

# INTERVIEW LIKE A PRO

The best interviewers are laser-focused on what they want. And they come to the interview prepared to get it. But they have a special way of doing this. They must get candidates to open up and show their true colors, which may come through in subtle clues that others may miss. Finally, the best interviewers don't come into an interview with preconceived notions about a candidate. They are open-minded and eager to learn—and give everyone an opportunity to let their talents shine.

## PREPARE TO SUCCEED

There are several things that you need to do to prepare for an effective interview. The first is preparing to speak with the candidate about your company. Make sure that you are ready to discuss your mission, vision, and values, in addition to company culture, benefits, and perks.

The next level of preparation is for the role itself. Make sure that you know which talents and skills you are looking for and have standardized questions to evaluate for them. You should also have an accompanying scorecard for each interview.

Take time to review the candidate's application—resume, cover letter, prescreen questions, assessment reports, and notes from any previous interviews (such as a phone screen). I also like to review a candidate's online presence, particularly their Linke-dIn profile (if they have one). I am looking for consistency with what appears on their resume, connections to people I know, and overall professionalism. I also love to read recommendations that they have received and given to others. Know what concerns you have about the candidate upfront and prepare to address them in the interview.

In addition to your own preparation, you should help the candidate prepare by sharing information on your interview process and who the candidate will be meeting with. We also like to send additional information to candidates outside of what is on our website, such as our vision statement. Candidates should know exactly what to expect. No surprises.

## HELP CANDIDATES BRING THEIR BEST

You should care about every candidate who interviews with you. It will improve the candidate experience and help you build a reputation as a great place to work. Plus, it's just the right thing to do. Regardless of whether they get an offer, you want every candidate to feel good about their interaction with you and your company.

There's another reason to help candidates feel comfortable: you want them to be themselves and show you everything that they have to offer. If your interview vibe is overly formal or intimidating, people will not be completely open with you.

Start every interview on a positive note. Give candidates a minute to get settled in the interview room and offer them a drink. Start on time and lead with a smile. Take a few minutes to introduce yourself and your role. Help candidates understand the role and why you are hiring for it. Show them that you prepared for the interview by mentioning something personal that you noticed on their resume. This is a great way to build rapport upfront and get candidates to open up to you. You want the interview to feel like a naturally flowing conversation, but it's hard to achieve that if you jump right into Q&A.

## REALLY LISTEN

When it's time for the interview, make sure that you really listen to candidates. Take notes. Make eye contact. Summarize what you've heard. It seems simple, but it's easy to get stuck in your own head instead of listening to what the candidate is saying. There have been plenty of times when I've had to tell myself to stop thinking about the great question that I'm going to ask next.

Think of someone in your life who has done an excellent job of listening to you. Someone who was truly present for you. Remember how that made you feel. That is how you want every candidate to feel. In addition to making candidates feel valued, focused listening will allow you to pick up on subtle things that you may have otherwise missed. You don't learn anything about the candidate when you're doing all the talking. The best interviewers make the conversation at least 90% candidate and at most 10% interviewer.

Try to listen slowly. Wait a few seconds longer than normal before asking your next question. This has helped me stay in the moment and not think about what I am going to ask next. It also creates a slower and more naturally flowing conversation, which candidates appreciate more than an interrogation. This extra pause after their initial response can also be magical. Usually, a candidate will open up more and expand on what they are saying, or they will head in a different direction. I often learn more from these second answers than I do from the first ones.

Make sure that you save at least a quarter of the allotted interview time for the candidate to ask you questions. This is an important decision for them too, so you need to make time for this. Plus, it's a great opportunity to see how well they prepared for the interview. Pay close attention to the questions they ask you. They will help you see what they value and how they think. I've been in interviews that have totally changed my outlook on someone once we got to the questions section. Some for the better. Others for the worse!

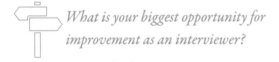 *What is your biggest opportunity for improvement as an interviewer?*

Every one of us has unconscious biases. These serve a purpose for humans and help us make quick decisions. But they can also lead to flawed hiring choices. Many interviewers only spend the first five minutes really interviewing someone. The rest of the time is spent confirming their bias and assumptions about the candidate. Don't let this happen to you.

Here are some examples of unconscious bias:

1. *Halo Effect* – This happens when you allow one obvious positive trait about a person to affect how we judge them in other unrelated areas. This single obvious positive trait serves as a kind of "halo" that causes people to make false assumptions about their abilities or personality.

2. *Horn Effect* – This is the inverse of the halo effect. Rather than a "halo" bestowing positive attributes to a person, the "horns" are perceived negative attributes that cause you to jump to negative (and equally inaccurate) conclusions about a person.

3. *Confirmation Bias* – This is the tendency to look for information that confirms a belief you already have and to subconsciously filter out all evidence to the contrary. This leads us to create flawed patterns in our thinking.

4. *Affinity Bias* – This describes our natural tendency to get along with people who are like us. It's easy for hiring managers to fall victim to affinity bias, especially when evaluating for culture fit.

There are ways to combat unconscious bias. Start by using a score-card and a list of interview questions. This will keep you focused on what really matters for the role. If possible, have more than one interviewer participate in the interview process. You will get the benefit of another person's perspective, who might interpret a candidate's answers differently than you.

 *Which type of bias are you most susceptible to having in the interview process?*

# KEEP YOUR SCORECARD SIMPLE

If you want your scorecard used consistently, then you need to keep it simple. I recommend listing the three main hiring criteria (Ability, Motivation, Culture Fit) and answer Yes or No to each one.

---

**Interview Scorecard**

A more detailed version of the scorecard would list out the top 2-3 requirements for Ability and each of your core values for Culture Fit:

**Ability**

| Skill/Talent #1 | Skill/Talent #2 | Skill/Talent #3 |
|---|---|---|
| [Yes/No] | [Yes/No] | [Yes/No] |

**Motivation** [Yes/No]

**Culture Fit**

| Core Value #1 | Core Value #2 | Core Value #3 |
|---|---|---|
| [Yes/No] | [Yes/No] | [Yes/No] |

**Final Determination**

| Ability | Motivation | Culture Fit |
|---|---|---|
| [Yes/No] | [Yes/No] | [Yes/No] |

---

Someone should have all three main hiring criteria as a Yes if they are going to be hired. There is no option for Maybe. You may not feel strongly about their ability for one of the requirements you listed, but you still need to make a call for ability: Yes or No. If you are not sure, then you may want to spend more time interviewing them or get another opinion.

If you are fortunate enough to have more than one great option for the position, compare the candidates objectively by focusing on ability, motivation, and culture fit. Each candidate will have different strengths and weaknesses. If two candidates are close in ability, give the advantage to the candidate who is stronger on motivation and culture fit.

Keep it objective, but recognize that your subjective judgment is going to be there no matter what. Sometimes this gut judgment can serve you well when you are on the fence with someone. But make sure that you don't stray far from the hiring criteria you wrote down when you started your search.

 *What is keeping you from using a candidate scorecard if you aren't already?*

# YOU ARE BEING INTERVIEWED TOO

Top performers can afford to choose. And they are interviewing you as much as you are interviewing them. If you show up to the interview unprepared and ask random questions as they come to you, then candidates will wonder what it would be like to work for you.

Most of all, you need to take a personal interest in candidates. Show them that you care and want to see them succeed in their job search. If they feel like they are being run through the process as another resume, then you won't create that connection. That connection, rather than money or anything else, is often the deciding factor that determines where a top performer chooses to work.

Don't forget to sell the right candidates on your opportunity. Talk about your mission and vision and how they can help you achieve them. Describe your culture and why people love to work at your company. Talk about the rest of the hiring process. Don't make the candidate ask about the next steps. And if you are ready to take a candidate to the next step, get it scheduled right then and there.

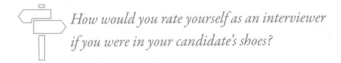 *How would you rate yourself as an interviewer if you were in your candidate's shoes?*

# MAKE THE RIGHT HIRE

COMMIT TO A PROCESS

TRUST, BUT VERIFY

THE CANDIDATE DEFENSE

THE OFFER

CLOSE THE DEAL

CELEBRATE THE HIRE

# COMMIT TO A PROCESS

Ability, motivation, and culture fit. These are the only things that matter when evaluating candidates.

There's no one right way to do this. Different roles (and cultures) will require different approaches. The one thing that we all must do is clearly understand who we are looking for and use a consistent process to identify the right person. You can use the Ideal Candidate Profile to organize your process.

Once you know what you need to measure and how you can evaluate it, designing the hiring process is straightforward. The tough part is deciding on the length of the process.

This doesn't have to be a lengthy process, but it may require more than you are doing right now.

You have a choice: you can either invest the time upfront and make the right hires consistently, or you can save time upfront by skipping steps and taking a gamble on whether a candidate will work out. In most cases, the time you save will be erased by the extra work you will have to do to manage, and ultimately replace, the wrong hires.

If you are hiring for frontline positions, as many of our clients do, you definitely feel the pressure to keep the process short. You have openings that need to be filled yesterday, and you feel like you don't have the time or luxury of being selective.

But you do. If you operate in an industry with high turnover, the opportunity for an improved hiring process to impact your results is huge! Imagine if you could be even just 10% better at hiring. That reduction in turnover would have a big impact on your growth and profitability. And 10% is a low target.

Here's how I would approach designing the hiring process at a high level. The goal is to invest the right amount of time for the right stage in the hiring process. Try to keep the early stages short so that you can spend more time with the right candidates later in the process.

## APPLICATION REVIEW

When I review an application, I want to know whether this candidate meets the basic criteria for the position. This will vary for an entry-level versus experienced role, but generally, I want to see that this person has the ability or potential ability to succeed. I also want to know whether the candidate's work preferences match the needs of the position. For example, a candidate must be willing to work evenings and weekends if that is what the position requires. Prescreen questions are a great way to determine this prior to an interview.

## INITIAL SCREEN

Candidates who pass the application review should be invited to have an initial conversation conducted over the phone. Keep these short, 15 to 20 minutes. This gives you enough time to evaluate someone's potential ability, motivation, and culture fit at a high level. All that you want to determine is whether you want to bring them in for an interview. This works well as a first step: neither you nor the candidate needs to commit to a formal interview yet. This generates a better response to your invitations and saves you time.

## INTERVIEW

This is the toughest part to organize. You will need to decide whether you want to have one round of interviews or two. Avoid conducting more than two rounds of interviews, or you may lose candidates to employers with shorter hiring processes. For frontline roles, one round of interviews is ideal. This will give you enough time to do a Lifeline Interview (or something similar) and allow the candidate to speak with your team and see what it's like to work there.

You will likely need two rounds of interviews if you have several people who need to be involved in the process, or if you want to give a more extensive job simulation.

If you include an assessment in your hiring process, you can either give it before the initial screen or between the initial screen and the interview. There are pros and cons to each approach, but I have found that more candidates will be willing to complete the assessment for you after you have had a conversation with them.

The most effective thing about your hiring process is that it's a process. Like any process, it's only effective if you stick with it consistently. That means that every candidate goes through the same process. This is the only way that you will be able to produce consistent results.

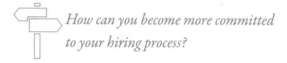 *How can you become more committed to your hiring process?*

Check out our *Hiring Process Design Worksheet* on **howtohire.com**

# TRUST, BUT VERIFY

This may be the most neglected stage in the hiring process. When people look back at hires that didn't work out, they usually regret not completing these steps. Reference checks and background checks take a little extra time and money to conduct, but they are worth it. You won't know how much they are truly worth until they help you avoid a bad—potentially devastating—hire.

I let candidates know upfront that we conduct reference checks and ask if they are able to provide them. This sets the tone and helps keep candidates honest during the hiring process. We always ask for at least three references. I would much rather speak with previous supervisors than co-workers, but sometimes this can get tricky. When a candidate is currently employed, you may not be able to get a reference from their current supervisor. Some companies, particularly large corporations, have a strict policy against managers providing references for previous employees. The best you can do in that case is to contact their human resources department, which should be able to at least verify their dates of employment.

Take a look at their employment history and compare that with the references they provided. If they recently worked somewhere for three years and don't have anyone besides a friend to serve as a reference, that would make me suspicious. Don't be afraid to ask them for better references, particularly supervisors, and see how they react.

When I conduct reference checks, I ask similar questions to the interview so that I can check for consistency:

- *When did she work for you?*
- *What were her responsibilities?*
- *What did she accomplish?*
- *What are her strengths?*

Don't ask about weaknesses. At least, not directly. People usually don't want to keep someone from getting a job, and providing a list of their weaknesses seems like a good way to do that. I like to frame the question a different way:

*What are some of the areas where you provided coaching/professional development while she worked for you?*

This puts the manager in a spot where they feel obligated to provide some feedback since it was their job as a manager to provide coaching and professional development. Another way to frame this question is:

*What kind of tasks did she enjoy doing the most? Which ones seemed less interesting to her?*

Reference checks do more than help you verify a candidate's employment history. They also allow you to speak with their manager to learn about their performance and get advice on the best ways to lead this person. My favorite question to ask in a reference call is:

*How can I be the best leader possible for this person?*

You can learn so much from the responses.

One hidden value with reference checks is that they could end up being a recruiting opportunity for you. High-quality candidates associate with other high-quality employees. If you speak with a candidate's former colleague as a reference, you may be able to recruit them to work for you—or at least leave a great impression on them, so they tell other people about your company. Always be recruiting!

Background checks can alert you to a candidate's criminal history. It's much better for you to find out at this stage rather than while they're on the job. You only need to make this mistake once to learn your lesson the hard way. Hopefully, that lesson won't cost you your business, as it has for some owners who have had employees embezzle money or harm customers/employees.

Not all background checks are created equal. Be sure to work with an accredited provider to determine the right package for you. Many employers choose to give an offer that is subject to the satisfactory completion of a background check. This limits the background checks they need to run to candidates who have accepted an offer.

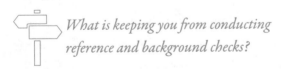 *What is keeping you from conducting reference and background checks?*

---

Check out our *Guide to Reference and Background Checks* on **howtohire.com**

---

# THE CANDIDATE DEFENSE

Once we are ready to make an offer, the manager responsible for the open position presents the case for hiring a particular person to our leadership team. We call this meeting the *Candidate Defense*.

The Candidate Defense is an important final step: a culmination of all the previous steps. It ensures that all previous steps in the process were followed and that the hiring manager has seriously considered the pros/cons of hiring this person. The group participating in the meeting is not there to approve or deny the hire; they are there to provide additional perspective to the hiring manager. They can help the hiring manager see their blind spots with this candidate, which is incredibly valuable.

In advance of the Candidate Defense, the hiring manager completes our standard defense form and sends this out along with supporting information, such as the resume, assessment reports, and interview notes. The defense form captures what is required of the position and how the candidate fits these criteria as well as our company core values.

The Candidate Defense helps managers identify the biggest concerns about hiring someone. It should also make the manager think about reasons why the candidate will not be successful in the position, as well as reasons that they might leave even if they perform well in the role.

Even if you are the business owner who is making the hire, I encourage you to use some form of a Candidate Defense. We use it for every hire, and it has saved me from major mistakes when I was so excited about a candidate that I was not seeing the full picture. Sometimes I have figured this out by working through the defense document. Other times, I have had people that I trust help me see something that I missed.

The Candidate Defense could be presented to your existing team. If you don't have the right team for that, then I suggest that you conduct it with another business owner or mentor. The important thing is that you take a step back and reflect before making a hiring decision.

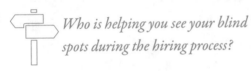

*Who is helping you see your blind spots during the hiring process?*

---

Check out our *Candidate Defense* template on **howtohire.com**

---

# THE OFFER

You have made it this far; now, it's time to make the best candidate a compelling offer to join your team. Here are the key elements that we discuss in our offers:

## COMPENSATION

Much like any big transaction, you don't want any surprises when it's time to close the deal. Now is the time to reiterate everything that you have talked about throughout the process. There should be nothing new introduced at this stage. Even with compensation. Especially with compensation.

We take an open and straightforward approach with compensation. We start by listing it on every job posting. Then Natalie, our People leader, shares the exact compensation with every candidate on the phone screen and confirms that this works for them, as we don't negotiate. This helps us be more equitable and ensures that there are no surprises when we get to the offer stage. The candidate knows exactly what they'll see on the offer letter. Candidates really appreciate it, and it helps us convert almost every offer we make into a hire.

I was skeptical about this approach at first, as I was used to paying people based on an improvement of their previous earnings. I'm glad that Natalie pushed us to change this, as I now see the flaws in my old approach. People who are qualified for the job deserve to get paid what we deem to be a fair amount for that role, regardless of their compensation history. Not more, and certainly not any less.

## BENEFITS

I would rather come in strong on benefits and not pay at the top of the market for compensation. Benefits can help define your culture. The top three for us are healthcare, retirement, and paid time off. We didn't always have great benefits. I made the investment over time, starting with healthcare. At first, we provided a stipend for employees to pay for their own healthcare insurance plans. This was okay to start, but I knew that we had to step up if we were going to become a truly great place to work. Plus, I simply wanted to do more for my team. We took a huge leap forward when we added a company health insurance plan and paid for 100% of employees' premiums (and 50% of premiums for their families). This felt like a big risk financially when we did it, but I knew it was the right decision immediately from the morale boost and appreciation I received from our team.

## WORK-LIFE BALANCE

We make it clear to candidates that we all have lives outside of work, and we want them to have the same. This is often the #1 consideration for candidates, particularly those with families. They will already have learned what an average workday and workweek looks like in the interview process. This is where we reiterate the value of working for us rather than the company that is going to pay you more but regularly expects you to work nights and weekends.

Part of work-life balance is flexibility. We trust people to get things done; what time and where it gets done is up to them. We make that clear when we make offers. I have found that when you hire the right people and give them this flexibility, you actually get more out of them than you ever would if you forced them to work certain hours. We don't have set hours except for client-facing roles, such as our support team, where we have made promises to be available to our clients at certain times.

## PROFESSIONAL DEVELOPMENT

The last area we cover when making an offer is professional development. The best candidates are going to want to see how this position will help them grow professionally. They will often turn down a job that pays more if they see a path to growth at your company. Show them what they will learn by working with you and what a potential growth path could look like for them. This is what gets the top performers really excited.

I recognize that it is challenging to offer benefits like these for certain positions, particularly hourly ones. But don't let that be an excuse—it's actually an opportunity. If it's challenging for you, then it will be challenging for other companies competing for the same talent. It's not all about how much you can spend. Think about how you could get creative with some new perks, and improve the way you talk about the great stuff you already do. Remember that these benefits will help you retain your current team, too. Think about the value of being able to keep high performers on your team for the long run. That may create some room in the budget.

 *How can you improve your offer letters to highlight the total benefits and compensation package?*

# CLOSE THE DEAL

The delivery of your offer is just as important as the offer itself. Don't mess it up by getting sloppy at the end!

In terms of the actual offer itself, I like to make a big deal about this. We create a formal offer letter and put together a benefits folder for them to review. Then we walk them through each section and cover all of the key areas: compensation, benefits, work-life balance, and professional development.

Before we all started working remotely, we asked people to come to the office to receive the offer in person. I want to be able to see how they react when they read the offer. This is much different than giving an offer over the phone. For remote hires, we do a video call and send the candidate an email with the offer package at the start of the call so that we can review it together, "face-to-face."

If you have communicated openly with candidates throughout the hiring process, then you should have an understanding of what is important to them. You need to use this information and show them how you will meet these needs. Candidates often sign on the spot. There will be some candidates who want to think about it and perhaps discuss it with their partner. I always accommodate these requests, but I ask them when they can get back to me with a response—preferably the next day. If I am sensing some hesitation, then I usually ask them about the pros/cons that they are weighing in their heads. I also ask about other offers that are outstanding or may be coming. Not everyone is forthcoming with these details, but you would be surprised by how many are.

Beware of candidates who seem to have a singular focus on money. These are the ones who will leave you as soon as a better offer comes along.

You won't win them all, but you should be able to learn something from each one. Sometimes candidates decide to take another job for more money or a better title. Sometimes candidates will take advantage of you, like the person who only wanted our offer to negotiate a raise with his current employer. It happens.

Not everyone is going to be a match for your company and what you have to offer, but you can use this feedback to adjust your approach to be more competitive. A couple of years ago we started offering unlimited paid time off as a benefit, in part because we learned that not having it was putting us at a disadvantage with certain candidates. I had been hesitant to make this switch because I thought that people would prefer to have a fixed amount of vacation time that they knew they were able to take, rather than saying that it is "unlimited." My team made a good case for it, so we made the switch with one important caveat: we added a mandatory minimum amount of paid time off that every full-time employee is required to take each year. This addressed the issue I've seen come up at tech companies that offer "unlimited" time off but never really allow anyone to take it. I do think that it has helped us become more competitive with candidates and has been well received by employees.

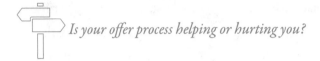 *Is your offer process helping or hurting you?*

# CELEBRATE THE HIRE

You have made your hire—now make sure that you take time to celebrate it! You and your team probably put a ton of work into this. Take a moment to thank each person who helped make it happen. Hiring is a big deal, and you want to make sure that your team knows that you feel that way. Take a deep breath and enjoy this moment. And remember that the work has just begun.

Most importantly, you want your new hire to know how excited you are. This person is no longer a candidate—their first employee experience is accepting your offer. What do you want their first impression to be? One of the benefits of bringing candidates into the office for the offer was that we got to parade them around once they accepted. Our team did a great job of making a big deal about this and giving out lots of high fives.

Have you ever been excited to buy something, only to be totally let down with the experience you have after the purchase? This happened to my wife and me recently when we bought a new truck. The sales representative was great throughout the sales process, as were the other people at the dealership. But then all of that went away after we made the purchase. No one was excited for us. And no one seemed to want to help us with a couple of questions we had. We almost returned the truck.

Don't let this happen to you. This is one of the top reasons that people quit within the first couple of weeks on the job (or just don't show up at all). The job they thought they took wasn't what it turned out to be.

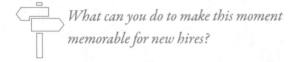 *What can you do to make this moment memorable for new hires?*

RETAIN

# RETAIN FROM DAY ONE

THE #1 RECRUITING STRATEGY

EVERYONE DESERVES A GOOD MANAGER

RETENTION STARTS WITH ONBOARDING

INVEST IN EARLY SUCCESS

YOU OWE THEM FEEDBACK

TIME NOW OR TIME LATER?

# THE #1 RECRUITING STRATEGY

Recruiting is hard. It's expensive and a huge distraction. And a lot of it doesn't even need to happen.

**The #1 recruiting strategy is retention.**

Hire the right people and do everything you can to keep them. When you retain your employees, you can focus on growing your business. Every time you have to replace a team member, it's an opportunity to upgrade. But it's also a step backward.

The cost of turnover is high—thousands of dollars even for your most entry-level employee. And that does not factor in the opportunity costs: how much could you have grown if you kept your team together?

If you want to hire and retain the best employees, then you cannot just give them a job. You need to help them build a career. Many believe that this isn't possible for people who work hourly shifts, as many of our clients' employees do. But these are the people on the frontline for you. They are the ones that serve your customers and keep them coming back for more. They deserve an opportunity to build a career. And if you don't offer it to them, the best will leave and look for someone who will.

This doesn't mean that you need to pay everyone a salary, or even increase their hourly pay and improve benefits—although those things will help, and they will be more affordable if you can increase your profits with a high-performing team.

A career is about more than money. It's about feeling like you are a part of something special—knowing that the work you put in each week is making a difference in people's lives. It's about growth and achievement both professionally and personally. It's about being part of a winning culture and being recognized for your contributions.

This is how to develop employees for life—people who will always be loyal to you, even if they move on at some point in their career. If you show someone that you care about them and help them get what they want, they will never forget it. This is the best way to lead an organization. And it is the most profitable way. Your "career employees" will wow your customers and stay with you for the long run. And most of the hiring you will have to do will be to grow—not replace—your team.

Retention doesn't start on day one—it's actually earlier than that. During the hiring process, you set expectations for what it would be like to work for you and your company. Now your new employees are paying close attention to see if you meet these expectations.

Your goal should be to exceed them.

 *Do you have a recruiting problem or a retention problem?*

# EVERYONE DESERVES A
# GREAT MANAGER

Have you ever read a quote that hits you so hard that it knocks you off your feet? That's how I felt when I read this one by Dan Springer, the CEO of DocuSign:

*"Every employee deserves a great manager, and every manager deserves the tools to be great."*

I had been trying to find the right way to articulate this concept to my team and our clients, and Dan did it for me.

It might sound obvious to say that every employee deserves a great manager, but at the very least it's a reminder to us. Actually, it's more of a wake-up call!

There are lots of not-so-great managers out there, You may have one on your team. Or you may be one yourself! No offense: I was definitely one for a while.

This brings me back to the second part of the quote: Most not-so-great managers have not been given the tools to be great.

Don't get me wrong, there are plenty of bad managers who need to be relieved of their duties. These include selfish leaders who care more about themselves than their teams, as well as people who got pushed into management and really never wanted it in the first place.

But for the people who really want to become great managers—the ones who get energy by helping others succeed—they may be simply a tool or two away from being great. The rest of this chapter shares some of the most important tools and processes that every manager should have. Do these things well, and your chances of retaining your team will go way up.

Make sure that you set a high bar for your managers. Remember, a manager rarely builds a team with a higher Talent GPA than their own GPA. If you are settling for B and C managers, then that's the team you should expect to have.

 *How much have you invested in giving your managers (and yourself) the tools to be great?*

# RETENTION STARTS WITH ONBOARDING

Your new hire's first week sets the tone and trajectory for their time with you. This week could leave them thrilled about the decision they made to work for you, or it could raise doubts and lead them back to the job boards to look at other options. Here's how we make sure that week one is a great one.

Onboarding starts as soon as someone gets hired. We send them an email that gives them everything they need to know about their first day, from start time to dress code. The last thing we want is for someone to be embarrassed on their first day.

Our team starts working a week ahead of time to make each employee's first day as smooth as possible. This includes setting up the new hire's computer and workstation as well as planning their first week. We schedule one-on-one time with their new manager and other team members who will be involved in training. The last thing we want to do is make a new hire feel unwelcome because we were not prepared.

New hires then spend some time reviewing and completing the required new hires forms and other items on our onboarding checklist. These include standard forms like the I-9, W-4, and a direct deposit authorization, as well as some company-specific items, such as our employee handbook. We use our own onboarding software to keep this entire process paperless. We aim to keep the completion of new hire forms to less than an hour; the last thing you want to do on your first day at a new job is to spend the whole time alone filling out forms.

This is where onboarding ends for many companies. This is a huge mistake.

We believe that onboarding is much more than new hire forms. It's about connecting new hires with the company, the team, and their manager.

## COMPANY

First impressions matter. That's why we make sure to start an employee's first day with what matters most.

On day one, our People leader, Natalie, sits down with new hires before anything else and talks about CareerPlug's core values. These are on our website and in our hiring process, but we want new hires to understand how our values fit into our language and our daily actions. New hires need to know what we stand for before anything else.

We never want to lose touch with our roots. We want new hires to understand where we came from and how we got here. Before we became a remote company, our onboarding process included lunch with me at Tacodeli, a restaurant across the street from the apartment where I started CareerPlug. It was the perfect place for me to get to know them, provide a quick history lesson, and reiterate the importance of living our core values.

We try to make onboarding as fun as possible. That's why we ask new hires to watch a series of CareerPlug history videos we made a few years ago to celebrate our ten-year anniversary. Some of the videos were interviews with employees who had been around for a while. Others were skits recreating funny moments in our history, such as the time that Eric accidentally threw away our keys and then proceeded to climb into the dumpster to retrieve them! At the time, one of our core values was *Go Above & Beyond*. Enough said.

## TEAM

As important as it is for a new hire to know the job, they also need to know the people. On the morning of their first day, we would give new hires a detailed tour of the office and introduce them to everyone. Then we pay for lunch for new employees and their team so they got to know each other socially. Now that we work remotely, we schedule one-on-one video calls with their team, introduce the new hire to the company through our internal message board, and send out a "getting to know you" email that includes questions answered by the new hire (like their favorite hometown meal and where they'd like to travel on their next vacation).

Our training is designed to put new hires in front of as many different people as possible to learn about them and their roles. I want everyone at our company to understand what we do and how we make money. If we don't take the time to teach new hires these things, then we cannot expect them to make good business decisions for us.

Relationships matter. If new hires feel like they're part of a team, they're more likely to speak up and ask for help. And they're more likely to stick around.

## MANAGER

Some companies jump right into on-the-job training on the first day. That's not our approach to preparing someone for success in a role. We believe it's more important to establish a relationship between the new hire and their manager.

We schedule a meeting on the first day to set expectations. This is a critical conversation that sets the tone for their relationship. We have each person talk about how someone wins and loses with them and how to best address sensitive issues. The manager and employee then review the job description and training plan.

From there, the rest of the first week is pretty structured. We pack in a lot, but we also give new hires some space to breathe. They need time to process, review, and take it all in. In addition to detailed information about their role, we give new hires access to our internal training system. We created a new hire training course, which includes information about company policies and history, software that we use internally, as well as our applicant tracking system software used by our clients. We try to make it interactive and humorous so that new hires stay engaged. Remember, you want to get them excited about joining your team. Don't bore them!

Space is good, but be sure not to leave new hires to fend for themselves. Check in, answer questions, and be there for them.

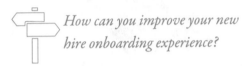

*How can you improve your new hire onboarding experience?*

---

Check out our *Onboarding Checklist* on **howtohire.com**

---

# INVEST IN EARLY SUCCESS

Each hire you make should give you leverage. They should make work easier for you and your other employees. But you cannot expect this to happen right away. You need to invest time into this person.

You need to teach them how to think. This is the only way that you will be able to set them free and allow them to act on your behalf.

I hired Jenny a few years ago to help me manage my growing workload as leader of the company. But I didn't want an assistant—I needed someone who could double me. Her title wasn't officially Chief of Staff, but that's what she was. We spent weeks talking about my schedule, my email, and the important people in my life. She shadowed me and asked a ton of questions. I took the time to explain everything to her in detail—not just the *what* and the *how*, but also the *why*. Soon she started taking small parts of my job away from me. Not long after that, she was doing large parts of my job for me, including managing some important projects.

Jenny excelled and took on additional leadership responsibilities as we grew, including a role leading all client-facing teams.

Recently, Jenny took over for me as President. She is now responsible for all internal operations at the company. This has allowed me to take on the role of CEO and focus externally on developing the strategies and relationships to grow our business.

This would not have happened if I had not invested a lot of time with her upfront.

It all started with a 90-day plan.

We use a 90-day training plan to map out a new hire's success. The objective of the plan is to have the new hire trained and performing in their role within 90 days. This does not mean that they have learned everything, but they should be producing by this point.

The plan is very detailed in the early stages, with specific tasks laid out in training checklists. After the first couple of weeks, the training plan transitions from a task checklist ("do these things") to one focused on milestones ("achieve these goals"). We want to ensure that new hires are proficient in certain aspects of the job by certain dates. The plans usually include a combination of quantitative and qualitative goals.

The 90-day training plan will not be successful unless managers and employees are discussing it regularly. This needs to happen at least daily for the first couple of weeks. Then it can shift to milestones. Each milestone has an associated checkpoint with a manager so that the new hire can celebrate wins, receive feedback, and work past obstacles. (We schedule these check-in meetings upfront so no one forgets about them.) The milestones become more spaced out over time until we reach the 90-day point.

HOW TO HIRE

If you hire the right person and invest in their early success, then you will likely have a long-term asset to help you grow your company. Does it always work out this way? No. Sometimes you invest a lot and get burned by someone leaving. This is frustrating, and it's easy to become cynical about making that upfront investment. But you will never reach your potential as a company if you don't.

Zig Ziglar said it best: "The only thing worse than training people and having them leave is not training people and having them stay."

 *How can you invest more into your employees' early success?*

---

Check out our *90 Day Plan* template on **howtohire.com**

---

# YOU OWE THEM FEEDBACK

I used to be terrible at giving critical feedback. Part of it had to do with being a naturally conflict-averse person. The other part is that I would blame myself for their performance issues. I did not set them up for success—at least, that was the story that I told myself.

Then one day, I got called out by one of my leaders. He told me that I owed him feedback and that was the only way that he was going to get better. He was totally right.

Feedback got easier for me after I read *Radical Candor* by Kim Scott. She uses a quadrant framework to teach the Radical Candor concept. To get into the Radical Candor quadrant, you have to 1) *Challenge Directly* and 2) *Care Personally*. I had the Care Personally part covered, but I was failing at Challenge Directly. That put me in a quadrant called *Ruinous Empathy*, which sounded terrible to me.

I was motivated to change and get myself out of that quadrant. The next week, I scheduled a meeting with an employee to have a tough conversation that I had been putting off for too long. I printed the quadrant and took it to the meeting to start the conversation. I explained to the employee that I cared about him and that I owed it to him to share how I was feeling and challenge him directly to improve.

Then I used a tactic that I learned from *Fierce Conversations* by Susan Scott. Before my meeting, I wrote a letter to this employee. The letter stated the issue, gave examples, and shared how I was feeling about it. Then I shared what was at stake, how I contributed to the issue, and my desire to resolve it. I read the letter in its entirety without interruption. Then I said that I wanted him to take a day to think about it; after that, we could meet again so that he could respond to me.

The letter technique worked so well for me because it allowed me to collect my thoughts in advance and control the conversation. In the past, I would have gone in with what I planned to say, only to get sidetracked as soon as the employee got defensive (or, more likely, I got nervous about delivering the feedback). With the letter, I just went for it. I remember being halfway through reading the letter and thinking to myself, "I cannot believe that I am saying this!"

I have only had to write feedback letters a handful of times when there was a major issue with someone. Otherwise, I just rely on the *Radical Candor* explanation to kick things off: "I care about you, and I want you to be successful. Therefore, I owe it to you to challenge you directly."

Make sure that you put even more energy into providing positive feedback to people. Reinforce what they are doing well. Show them that you notice how hard they are working. If you are good at noticing things that people are doing wrong, then you need to work at recognizing what they are doing right.

I have had to work at this as well. Heaping praise did not come naturally to me, partly because I don't seem to need it as much as some other people do. That is one of the most important lessons that I have learned as a leader: you have to be the leader that each of your employees needs you to be, not the leader that you would want for yourself. I don't need a lot of public recognition, but some of my people crave it. That means that I need to get up in front of the team and sing their praises when they deserve it.

I don't wait until formal performance reviews to deliver feedback. I put a lot of energy into those, but most of it is feedback—positive or negative—that I have already shared with my employees. My goal is for there to be no surprises when I give the reviews. I usually give my feedback during our weekly one-on-one meetings or directly after an event that created new feedback. If it's positive feedback, I will praise people in front of their peers (if that is how they like to be recognized). If it is negative, then I will pull them aside and address it as soon as possible.

Remember that you also need feedback to grow. Make sure that you have created open channels so that you can receive it. Ask people how you are doing and what you can do to improve. If you never get any constructive feedback, then you have not built enough trust with your team. There are other things that they are not sharing with you as well.

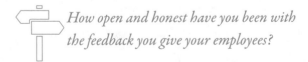 *How open and honest have you been with the feedback you give your employees?*

# TIME NOW OR TIME LATER?

I recently became a father. There's one lesson that has stuck with me: *to a child, love is spelled T-I-M-E.*

But it's also true for leaders. This stuff takes time.

You can either spend the time now. Building relationships. Connecting them with your purpose and values. Teaching them how to think. Or you can spend it later. Reposting your job—again! Filling in for missing people. Sifting through resumes and interviewing whenever you can squeeze it in.

No leader really *has* the time. But some choose to *make* the time.

The best thing that we've done to make the time at CareerPlug is build it into our processes and schedules. We've created a communication rhythm that, when it's working well, keeps everyone connected at the company. We had most of these meetings previously, but reading *Traction* by Gino Wickman really pushed us to synchronize everything across the company.

Every team at the company operates to the same rhythm. Each morning, teams start the day with a huddle. Every week, each team has a meeting and employees have one-on-one meetings with their managers. There are also a few weekly meetings with employees from different teams that work together frequently.

Every quarter, teams have offsite planning meetings—usually for a half or full day. Managers also have performance conversations with each employee.

We also send out anonymous employee satisfaction surveys quarterly. Then, we review the results as a leadership team and follow up with the company to address issues and themes that arise.

When you add it all up, this is a huge investment in time. It wouldn't happen if we didn't have it on the calendar. Not a one-time meeting—but a recurring event.

Maybe we do so much because we are in the people business.

But aren't we all?

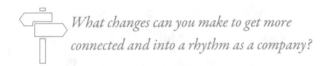 *What changes can you make to get more connected and into a rhythm as a company?*

# ENGAGE TO GROW

THE WORK OF YOUR LIFE

WHAT DRIVES YOUR TEAM?

GIVE AUTONOMY

BUILD MASTERY

INSTILL PURPOSE

HELP THEM GET WHAT THEY WANT

# THE WORK OF YOUR LIFE

Retaining your people is just the beginning. It may not feel like it right now, but that's a pretty low bar.

It's ultimately about reaching your potential. If you want to reach your potential as a leader, then you have to help your team reach theirs.

But what does that mean?

It comes down to helping people thrive and feel like they are doing the work of their lives. This was another concept from Dan Springer that opened my eyes. When you look back on your life and are proud of what you accomplished individually and as a team. Those moments . . . that's the work of your life.

It may seem lofty, but it's not. Especially when you are talking about frontline employees. Most have never experienced the feeling of having a career or being part of a winning team. Some have not even had the satisfaction of setting a personal growth goal and achieving it.

You have the potential—even responsibility—to help your people do the work of their lives.

If you don't, then they will eventually look for someone who will.

 *When you look back at your career later in life, what do you think you'll be most proud of?*

# WHAT DRIVES YOUR TEAM?

Motivation can be fickle. What happens when the excitement of the new job starts to fade? Is it time to move on to a new adventure? Or, perhaps worse, is it time to get comfy and hit cruise control?

I learned a lot about motivation by reading *Drive* by Daniel Pink. First, I got clear on the difference between *extrinsic* versus *intrinsic* motivation.

Extrinsic motivation drives people to perform an activity to earn a reward (or to avoid punishment). It's a force that influences from the outside.

Intrinsic motivation drives people to perform an activity for its own sake—for personal satisfaction. It comes from the inside.

Which one works best in the workplace? It's usually a combination of the two and depends on the type of work being done. But a couple of things were clear to me:

1. *Extrinsic motivation can be overdone.* This is why you have to know your team. In some cases, excessive rewards may have the opposite effect and sap someone's intrinsic motivation.
2. *There's no such thing as too much intrinsic motivation.* Think about your greatest accomplishments in life. I bet they've come from a deep, burning desire within you. Not from something on the outside.

I remember thinking that there were only two ways you can manage someone: with a carrot or a stick. I'm not a forceful person, so I thought I was a carrot guy all the way. Looking back, I now see that these are both tools for extrinsic motivation—either to earn an external reward or to avoid punishment!

**If you really want to motivate someone, you have to do it with a heart.**

For me, that means showing that you care. When you care about them, they'll care about you (and your business). Sure, there will be some employees who will take advantage of you. But don't let those exceptions cloud your thinking on this.

You need to build a connection with your employees. But it's more than a personal connection. You need to build a fire inside of them. Fueled by intrinsic motivation.

Daniel Pink says there are three key drivers of intrinsic motivation in the workplace: *Autonomy, Mastery,* and *Purpose.* When you are doing this well, these are the messages that your employees hear from you:

Autonomy: *"I trust you and know that you will do the right thing."*

Mastery: *"I care about you and want to see you grow."*

Purpose: *"I need you and want us to accomplish our mission together."*

In the next few sections, I'll share the connections that I made between these intrinsic motivation drivers and what we're doing at CareerPlug. It's definitely a work in progress!

 *How do you motivate your team?*

# GIVE AUTONOMY

I've found that there are two types of people in the world: *trust givers* and *trust earners*.

A trust giver's mindset is *"I'm going to trust you until you give me a reason not to."*

With a trust earner, it's more like *"I'm not going to trust you until you give me a reason to."*

When you micromanage someone, either by constantly looking over their shoulder or setting highly restrictive policies, you are telling them that you don't trust them. Top performers won't go for this. They probably won't stick around. If they do, you won't get their best work.

I'm a trust giver. This doesn't mean that you cannot lose my trust. You definitely can, and my team would tell you it's hard to earn it back when that happens. It really comes down to this: how would I want to be treated if I was the employee?

Generally speaking, I think that CareerPlug relies more on core values versus policies. I would rather give our team some leeway and guideposts to make decisions instead of telling them what to do.

Teach them how to think. Don't do the thinking for them. Measure people by their results.

Just as this management style doesn't work for every type of manager, it doesn't work for every type of employee either. I've had some people work for me who didn't succeed because I gave them too much room to operate. They wanted me to tell them what to do. That's not my style. If I have to tell you exactly what to do, that often leads to me having to do your job for you. And that usually doesn't last long.

I also don't like to tell people when or where they need to work. Again, I really only care about the results.

Top performers love this flexibility. Maybe they have a family obligation every Tuesday and Thursday afternoon. Maybe they prefer to start work earlier or end later to be more productive, which might include reducing their commute. Maybe they want to have a focus day with no internal meetings or interruptions. I've always found that the more you give top performers, the more you get in return. Your biggest challenge will probably be making sure that they take enough breaks and don't burn out. This is a real risk if you don't work with your employees to set limits.

You may be thinking: *"That's fine for a tech company like yours, but this kind of autonomy wouldn't work for my company."*

You may be right. But not completely.

We have more flexibility with how we work compared to most companies. Our most restricted group is probably our support team since they have set hours that they need to work to be available to help our clients. But even with groups that are more tied down to a location or schedule, there are opportunities for autonomy.

We have *response time* goals for how quickly we respond to clients, but we don't have *call time* goals. Our reps can take as much time as they need. Sometimes that could impact us hitting our response time goals, but we'd rather have a short-term increase in response time over an all-the-time micromanaging of how they take care of clients.

We do set standards for call quality, but we don't make reps use scripts. Our managers have a quality monitoring process and grade a sample of calls each day. We provide coaching to our reps to help them improve, but we don't tell them what to say. We trust that the best way for our reps to take good care of our clients is to let them be themselves.

Some people think that you cannot operate well with autonomy. I think you cannot operate well without it.

The best companies trust their frontline employees to take this even further. Ritz Carlton is the gold standard for quality service. Ritz empowers its employees to spend up to $2,000 to solve a customer's problem. No manager approval required. Talk about trust! This number may sound absurd for your business, but it's not for theirs. Their average customer spends over $250,000 with them over their lifetime. Given that context, it might be the same as you allowing employees to solve a problem by comping a meal at your restaurant or giving someone a free month at your gym.

It's a smart investment to make for your customers. But it's an even better one for your employees.

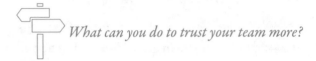 *What can you do to trust your team more?*

One of our core values is *Keep Growing*. We look for lifelong learners in our hiring process, so I know how important this is to our team. For a long time, we relied mostly on our individual employees to take initiative to learn. We were always encouraging when employees asked us to help them grow—we've even helped pay for tuition/program expenses in some cases. But I knew that we needed a more proactive, organized approach. We took on this challenge from a couple of angles: company-wide and individual.

First, we made a commitment to help everyone at the company become a *Hiring Expert*. We realized that our clients are often small business owners who do not have a recruiter or HR professional on their team. They rely on us for our expertise, and we are eager to help. This was one way that we differentiate ourselves from other hiring software companies.

Another reason why the Hiring Expert title was important to me: I wanted to give our team, our support team in particular, a path toward mastery. Our support team has grown with our client base, and we now help hundreds of clients per day with a variety of questions and issues. But I've always resisted calling that team a "call center." That term reminds me of a low-end, transactional job without much upward mobility. That's not the kind of position that I want to have at CareerPlug. And it's not the kind of experience that I want to provide our clients when they need our help.

What you call things at the company matters. Pay attention to that. But a name only goes so far. You have to show the team that you mean it and truly make it better.

We built a Hiring Expert training program to create a path toward mastery. This was a big investment of time, but I'm glad that we did it. It had the added advantage of pulling all of our teams together to work toward a common goal. And the great news is that we've been able to make most of this training material directly available to our clients to consume themselves.

The Hiring Expert program was an important step toward mastery, but we still needed to do more to help each individual grow in their own careers. Each of our employees has a growth plan that charts a course for their professional development. It starts with a long-term goal and breaks that down into short-term goals. Then it examines the skills needed to accomplish these goals. All of that was great, but we were missing a process to make ongoing progress on these plans. They were collecting dust!

I found a solution to this challenge when I read *The Sales Acceleration Formula* by Mark Roberge. The author led the sales team at Hubspot, a fast-growing marketing software company. But what really intrigued me about Mark was his background—he has a degree in Mechanical Engineering. In his book, Mark details all of the processes that he built for his teams. The one that stood out to me was around ongoing skill development.

Like most great processes, this one was simple. At the start of each month, an employee and their manager create a goal for one skill the employee wants to develop for that month. Sometimes the manager will prescribe a goal if they see a deficiency or specific opportunity, but usually, the employee has some autonomy to choose. Employees update managers on their progress each week. At the end of the month, they review the goal and determine whether it was met. Then they set a new goal for the next month. Everyone does this on the same day. The following day, managers meet with their leader to report on the progress made by their team in the previous month, as well as the skill goals set for the upcoming month.

There are three things about this process that make it work well:

1. **Focus** - Employees only *focus* on one goal at a time. You cannot focus on two things at once. Try it with your eyes. Even if the two things are right next to each other, you can only focus on one of them. The same thing goes for skill development. If you are not focused on one thing, then you are not focused on anything.

2. **Routine** - Everyone in the company is working on skill development consistently using the same routine.

3. **Accountability** - The extra step of having managers report their team's results up to their leader is critical for companies that have a middle management layer.

We have adopted this skill development program with one adjustment: we use a quarterly cycle instead of monthly. This allows employees to go deeper into a specific skill.

Imagine how strong your team would be if everyone made at least four major skill improvements per year—especially if you could keep the same team together long term. You would be unstoppable!

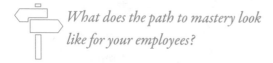 *What does the path to mastery look like for your employees?*

# INSTILL PURPOSE

You cannot spend too much time connecting your team's work with your purpose. Our team is clear on ours: empower people to reach their potential by making it easier for business leaders to hire and develop the right people. The challenge is how to communicate the impact our team is making.

I got some inspiration from an anecdote in *The Culture Code* by Daniel Coyle. One chapter profiles work that Adam Grant, an author and organizational psychologist, did to improve the results for a student-led fundraising team at the University of Michigan. Getting donations from alumni was tough. There was a 93% rejection rate. The university tried several incentive contests (read: extrinsic motivators), but none of them worked.

Grant took a different approach. He wanted to connect the team to the impact they were making. First, he shared a letter from a student who had received a scholarship funded by alumni donations. The student talked about how he has always dreamed of going to the University of Michigan, and it would not have been possible without this scholarship. Next, he invited other scholarship recipients to come and share similar heartwarming stories in person.

Grant's approach worked. Student fundraisers spent 142% more time on the phone and increased donations by 172%! He connected them to their team's purpose and showed how they were making an impact. Pure intrinsic motivation.

We have experimented with different ways to connect our team with the impact they are making. Our best results have come from collecting client success stories and sharing them around the company. It only takes one hire to make a huge difference in a small business, and I love to hear from our clients when they hire a great one.

As the number of hires made across our system grows each year, I've tried to find creative ways to show the magnitude of it. Cities and stadiums seem to work well: *"This year, our clients hired over 100,000 people using CareerPlug. With all of that talent, we could have filled the entire Rose Bowl or built a city the size of Asheville, North Carolina!"*

Don't forget that the *Why* of what your company does is more important than the *What* or *How*.

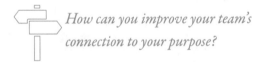 *How can you improve your team's connection to your purpose?*

# HELP THEM GET WHAT THEY WANT

To get the most out of employees, you need to know what *they* want and help them get it. This is why I love to hire highly motivated people. They want more out of their lives, and they are willing to work for it.

The Lifeline Interview that we conduct during the hiring process documents what a person wants to accomplish personally and professionally in the next three years. This is so powerful because it shows you what matters most to them in life. They took your job because they believed that it would help them accomplish these things. They will probably leave if they stop believing this.

But there was a problem. We were not doing enough to help our employees get what they wanted out of life. We had a process in place, but it wasn't an action plan.

I was inspired to do more after reading *The Dream Manager* by Matthew Kelly. It's a story about a fictional janitorial company that transformed their business—and significantly reduced turnover—after creating a program to help employees realize their dreams.

The first adjustment I made was to start using the term *dreams*. I think it sets employees at ease and makes them more open to sharing with you.

To get started, it's important to review the dream list they came up with during the Lifeline Interview to see if any adjustments are needed. I like to wait 90 days from their start date before doing this. New hires should be focused on getting up to speed and performing in their role for at least that long.

If you did not have them do this during the hiring process, then you can take them through the forward-looking section of the Lifeline Interview to capture an initial dream list.

We help employees take their dreams and think through the milestones they need to reach to achieve them. Then we have them set 1-2 quarterly goals to move things in the right direction. *The Dream Manager* recommends that you hire a Dream Manager to manage the program. We didn't start with one; we thought that it would be more practical to have our managers fill that role with help from our People leader. But when we made a commitment to center our culture around personal growth and development, we knew that we needed to have a dedicated person in this seat. Fortunately, one of our Partner Success Managers, Amy, was interested in shifting her career toward coaching—so she has become our first People Development Manager.

It is important to revisit the goals set in the Lifeline Interview once a year to see whether they are still valid. People's goals change over time, especially after major life events. This is also a good time to see how this person is progressing with these goals. People naturally reflect on their jobs when they have a work anniversary. This would be a great time to review goals and progress.

Not everyone will be ready to work on their growth and dreams with you. You should make this optional. I had a mentor teach me an important lesson when it comes to helping others grow. People are operating in one of three places: *dysfunctional, functional,* or *optimal.* You cannot help a dysfunctional person go directly to optimal. They need to get to functional first. For dysfunctional employees, this probably means you need to help them get the basics down: show up on time, do your job, live our values. You cannot help them get what they want until they start getting you what you need from them.

Sometimes people's goals change and the job you have for them no longer aligns. Or perhaps you have taken them as far as you can and they are ready for a new challenge, such as starting their own business. I never like to lose good people, but I don't want to get in the way of people chasing their dreams. Reading *Superbosses* by Sydney Finkelstein changed my perspective on this. The book showcases leaders from various fields who have become super-bosses, people who help others accomplish more than they ever thought possible. Many people who grow under a superboss become highly respected leaders themselves, often leaving to take on bigger challenges. If you only hire people who you think are going to work for you forever, are you hiring the best talent possible?

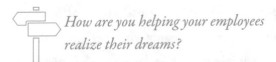 *How are you helping your employees realize their dreams?*

Check out our *Growth Plan* template on **howtohire.com**

# IT ALL COMES BACK TO CULTURE

MAKE RELATIONSHIP DEPOSITS

SHOW GRATITUDE

BUILD COMMUNITY

DO SOMETHING THEY WILL NEVER FORGET

# MAKE RELATIONSHIP DEPOSITS

I think about every important relationship in my life as having a bank account. You can make deposits and withdrawals. The balance can be a healthy surplus or a dangerous deficit. Every interaction you and your leaders have with your employees is either a deposit or withdrawal.

Stop by their desk to say hello and ask about their family. *Deposit.*

Recognize them in front of their team for a job well done. *Deposit.*

Trust them to take the lead on an important project. *Deposit.*

Cancel their one-on-one meeting with you with no notice. *Withdrawal.*

Make a joke at their expense in front of others. *Withdrawal.*

Micromanage them. *Withdrawal.*

Much like your real bank account, it usually takes a lot of small deposits over time to build a healthy account balance. It can come crashing down much faster with huge withdrawals.

Noted psychologist John Gottman first studied the relationship between positive and negative interactions in marriages, and he found the *magic ratio* (as he dubbed it) was five positive interactions for each negative one. Gottman used this ratio while observing 700 newlywed couples to predict who would divorce with 94% accuracy. I believe that the same principle holds true with any relationship.

Deposits and withdrawals happen on both an individual and company level. You cannot expect to have healthy individual balances unless your company culture is in a healthy place. Company changes like laying off or firing employees can be big withdrawals, even for employees who are not directly affected.

The deposits and withdrawals go both ways. Your employees may deplete their balance with you by neglecting their work or treating others poorly. It is important to monitor this, but you need to focus on what you are contributing to the relationship.

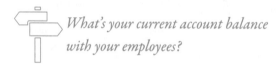 *What's your current account balance with your employees?*

# SHOW GRATITUDE

One of the best ways to make relationship deposits is through recognition and gratitude. This is such a valuable deposit that you can make, and it does not cost you a thing! In spite of that, gratitude is one of the first things to disappear when people get busy. This was so important to us that we built in a few mechanisms to make gratitude routine at the company.

We have a company-wide meeting every Friday afternoon, and the main purpose is to celebrate the week and give *Shout Outs* to each other. Employees take turns recognizing someone else from the team. The employee giving the Shout Out often references one of our core values, which I love since it reinforces what we value in our culture.

We also have a Shout Out channel on our internal message board for people to recognize people at any time for a core value, usually accompanied by a fun GIF animation!

We added an item to the end of our weekly leadership agenda: Gratitude. We end each meeting by recognizing someone at the company who exemplified our core values over the past week. A leader can nominate someone and share a quick anecdote, then another leader volunteers to follow up with this person to thank them. It's a great way to end our meeting. Plus, it gives our leadership team at least one person per week to contact and share our gratitude!

We also make a big deal about people's work anniversaries (or "workiversaries") with us. Our People leader, Natalie, came up with the idea of a workiversary prize wheel. Each Friday at the company meeting, people with a workiversary get to spin the prize wheel while being cheered on by the rest of the team. The prizes include gift cards, movie tickets, free lunch or dinner, and everyone's favorite, the mystery prize, when Natalie surprises a lucky employee with a gift that she buys based on things that they like.

Each year we have two company parties—a holiday party in December and the Pluggies in June. The Pluggies is a celebration of CareerPlug's birthday (June 21). The first Pluggies was held at Chili's and was sort of us mocking the Dundies episode from *The Office*. I bought a bunch of the plastic wall plates that go around electrical outlets and created Pluggie "awards" for every employee. Each one was a personalized attempt at humor by me—things like "Most likely to have the most consecutive days wearing a plaid and/or pearl snap shirt" (awarded to Walter). It was a funny thing that gave each employee some recognition and showed them that I knew something about them.

This became harder for me to keep up with as we grew. Recently, we shifted responsibility for creating Pluggies to our managers. We also stopped giving these out one by one at the Pluggies party, since it took way too long. Instead, we started giving out Core Value Awards. There is one award for each of our core values, which includes a nice plaque and a cash bonus. Our employees nominate their peers for each core value, then our leadership team picks a winner and runner-up from each group. The Pluggies is our biggest event of the year and a core part of our culture. It helps us hit on two areas that are key to our culture: *Show Gratitude* and *Build Community*.

 *What can you start doing to show more gratitude?*

# BUILD COMMUNITY

People want to feel like they are part of something bigger than themselves. This gives them energy and motivates them to contribute. And it keeps people committed to your company. We put a lot of effort into building community at CareerPlug.

We do so much more than the company-wide meetings and annual parties that I've already discussed. It might be easier to start by describing what we *don't* do.

We don't call ourselves a family. We care about each other, but we are not a family. I want people to leave work so that they can be with their families and friends. Plenty of employees spend time together outside of work, but that is their choice—not a work function. Lines get blurry when you start talking about employees like family.

We don't have ping pong tables and kegs of beer in the office. This never made any sense to me. I have been told by friends who work at places like this that most of that stuff is never used, that people are often judged for playing a game of foosball in the middle of the day. We hire people who want to work hard and end at a decent time to enjoy the rest of the day. We organize happy hours and other social events, but we are not a culture fueled by alcohol—this is dangerous on many fronts.

We do have fun with holidays and special events. People dress up for Halloween, and this past summer we had a Wellness competition with points for anything from going to run to enjoying a cup of tea. For many years, we also had a big celebration for Harry Potter's birthday (July 31). At first, I was scratching my head on this one, but I realized that most of our team absolutely loves Harry Potter, and they go all out for his birthday. I finally gave in and dressed up as one of the characters (Sirius Black). The diehards immediately figured out who I was and got a kick out of that.

Giving is a big part of our culture. My wife and I are foster parents and have a special place in our hearts for children who are in foster care. This has been a key part of our personal giving for years. One of the best decisions that I have ever made was to get my company involved in this cause. During the holidays, we get wish lists from local teens who are in foster care. Each one of our departments gets to choose a teen and go shopping for them. We really try to make these kids feel special and usually get them whatever they put on their lists. This includes stuff like iPads and Air Jordan sneakers, but we also get requests for some really unique things. Last year, we bought one teen a manual typewriter and an assortment of other quirky gifts. We had a lot of fun with that one. These underprivileged kids would have never gotten gifts like these, or perhaps any gifts at all, if it wasn't for our team.

We also started a scholarship program for teens in foster care who are attending college. Each year, we receive scholarship applications and our employees vote for the winner. It started out as the CareerPlug Scholars program, but we changed the name to Bright Angel Scholars so that other companies can participate. We are now able to give several scholarships each year.

HOW TO HIRE

I wanted our support of kids in foster care to spark our giving, but I did not want to limit it to that. CareerPlug matches any donations that employees make to non-profits. We also have charitable incentives tied to us achieving company goals. Recently, we made substantial donations to two charities chosen by our team. It was a great way to celebrate our strong performance in the quarter.

Part of our vision is to donate 1% of our annual revenue to charity. We achieved that for the first time in 2021, and it felt amazing! I know that everyone on our team is proud of the contributions they made to help us get here.

Our CareerPlug community was built by our employees, not by me. I did a few things myself, like the scholarships and the Pluggies, but the rest of it was my team. I encourage people to take initiative and give them small budgets to create special experiences. Employees can join committees, including the ones responsible for planning our events, as well as our giving and sustainability efforts. We also have a culture club that helps us monitor our health as a team, and employee resource groups to promote diversity and inclusion.

This is what has worked for us. And it didn't happen overnight.

Think about what would work for you and your culture. Better yet, challenge your team to do it.

 *What can you start doing to build community within your company?*

# DO SOMETHING THEY
# WILL NEVER FORGET

Nothing matters more than how you treat people. It's a lot easier to make small daily deposits than it is to make big ones.

But every once in a while, you will have the opportunity to do something really special for someone. Don't miss it.

When I think about my most loyal long-term employees, I can trace their loyalty back to something special that I did for them along the way. I supported them at a time when they were down or really needed it. I invested in them and showed that I believed in their potential. I gave them a shot.

Those bigger deposits have helped the company weather some tough times. People didn't always agree with me, but most of them stuck with me.

Now that we are bigger, I cannot have this kind of impact on everyone. At least, not directly. I need to rely on my leaders to make these deposits. The best thing that I can do is make sure that my account balance is healthy with them and give them what they need to succeed.

There's a quote by Maya Angelou that says it better than I can. (It also happens to be one of my wife's favorites.) "I've learned that people will forget what you said, people will forget what you did, but people will never forget how you made them feel."

Take a moment right now to think about how you can do something special for someone on your team. Now make a commitment to yourself to do it.

 *How can you make a big deposit with one of your key employees?*

# FINAL THOUGHTS

## EXPERIENCE IS EVERYTHING

In the end, it all comes down to experience.

If you want to build an exceptional team, you need to create exceptional experiences for everyone involved. Think about what each stakeholder in the hiring process needs and what you can do to improve their experience. Don't forget about yourself, either. You won't be able to reach your potential unless you make it easier for yourself!

## EXCEPTIONAL FOR CANDIDATES & EMPLOYEES

You won't truly succeed in hiring unless you give candidates what they need. When it comes to top performers, it's always a buyer's market. You need to make sure that qualified candidates want to buy what you are selling. Start by understanding their needs as buyers and the jobs that they need to do as part of their buying process.

Job seekers want an easy way to learn about your company, find relevant job openings, and apply to the jobs from their phones. Once they apply, candidates want to receive feedback on their application status, schedule and prepare for interviews, and receive an offer with information to determine whether it's the right fit. Once candidates are hired, they need to prepare for the first day, understand their roles and the rules of the organization, and get oriented with the company and connect with their teams. After onboarding, employees want to continue to grow in their roles and do purposeful work. And they want to be appreciated for it.

Don't forget that every candidate is a potential advocate for you. So is every current and former employee. If you provide a great experience, they will tell others about it. If you don't, they'll tell others about that too. Use this to create promoters, not detractors. It starts with the hiring process.

## EXCEPTIONAL FOR MANAGERS

No one succeeds alone, and you will not succeed in hiring and building a winning team without the help of others. The challenge is that they are busy helping you run your company. Plus, they may not have a great process to use. Start by understanding their needs as managers and the jobs that they need to do.

Managers want an easy way to post job openings, attract applicants, and receive notifications about new applicants from their phones. Once people apply, managers want to narrow the list down to the most qualified candidates, schedule/conduct interviews, and hire the right ones. Once hires are made, managers need to prepare them for their first day on their teams, understand what needs to be done to complete onboarding, and get them ready to start working as quickly as possible. After onboarding, they want a system to develop top performers and retain them as long as possible.

If you are doing all of the hiring yourself, then you should get your team involved. There is no reason that you need to be the one reviewing all of the applicants upfront and scheduling the interviews. Delegate this to a key team member so that you can focus on the later stages of the hiring process. They will probably do a better job of this than you since it will be an important responsibility for them.

If you are managing everyone yourself, think about what you could do if someone took some of that responsibility off of your plate. What could you do if you had more time to work on the business? Start looking for leaders on your team and make a plan to develop them.

If you already rely on your team to help with hiring and managing, talk with them about their experiences and how you can help them improve those. Every hour that you save them is another hour that they can spend with your customers.

## EXCEPTIONAL FOR LEADERS

As a leader, you need to set a vision for your team to become exceptional at hiring. Then you need to develop a playbook for them to execute on that vision. Your challenge is getting everyone aligned and executing together, which is even tougher for decentralized organizations. Start by understanding your needs as a leader and the jobs that you need to do to accomplish your hiring goals.

Leaders want to build their brands and their organizations' reputations as great places to work and drive applicant flow for open positions. When it comes to the hiring process, leaders want to produce predictable results and reduce turnover, have visibility into their hiring performance, and hold managers accountable to results.

When it comes to the onboarding process, leaders want to build a process to set up new hires for success from day one, give managers a system to prepare new hires to perform, and ensure that the company remains compliant.

Leaders want a system to keep everyone engaged and connected to the company's mission. They want everyone to work together as one cohesive unit—living the core values every day.

No matter what role you play in the hiring process, everyone wants an experience that:

1. Gives them the information they need when they need it,
2. Allows them to get things done quickly from any device, and
3. Gives them confidence that they are making the right decisions.

The investment you make into improving everyone's experience will come back to you in the form of better results and happier people. Remember that little changes can go a long way, so take time to listen to people and make small improvements. You reap what you sow!

# ADAPT OR PERISH

Things are going to change. You will either adapt and survive (and hopefully thrive), or you will perish. It's harsh. But it's true.

As I wrote this, the pandemic impacted every person and every business in the world. Many of our clients had to shut down operations. Some had to transform their businesses before they reopened. Others never reopened.

We had to adapt.

First, we had to help our clients get through this. We allowed all clients who were directly affected to freeze their accounts with us until they were ready to start hiring again. Next, we set up a program called Hire Up that allowed new clients to have access to our software at no cost for 60 days. This helped businesses who needed to rebuild their teams in advance of reopening (and generating cashflow). My #1 job as the leader, besides taking decisive action to adapt, was to support my team. I focused heavily on gratitude and mindset. My books on stoicism—particularly *The Daily Stoic* by Ryan Holiday—were invaluable.

We are fortunate that we can do our work virtually, and our shift to 100% remote work was seamless. I didn't realize this, but we had been inadvertently preparing for this for over a year. Many of our employees had been asking to work from home once a week, so we put a policy in place for them to do that. When we decided to shut down the office, everyone was ready to go.

I don't suspect that things will ever go back to the way they were. Remote work, where it's possible, will become more accepted. We have decided to remain a remote company permanently. There are tradeoffs to this decision—collaboration and connection in general have been challenging. But there are also advantages. We're now able to hire the best talent from all over the country. And no one has to spend two hours per day commuting to the office anymore. They can now spend that time with their families. That makes me smile.

When I review our vision, I can see us still getting to the same destination—just through a different path.

When I read our core values, I see us still living them—in some ways more than ever.

At times, the slow changes scare me more than the immediate ones. It's easier to avoid them—to kick the can down the road. Then a major event happens that makes you realize that you should have gotten started sooner. The pandemic had a way of accelerating changes that were already happening; those who fared best were the ones who had already started to adapt.

One change has become crystal clear to me: People have changed the way they think about work. They are more selective now. Many are no longer willing to take a job with no potential. They want a shot at a career, and they want to work at an organization with a winning culture.

This is a threat to your business, particularly if you depend on frontline workers.

Get out in front of it and you may be able to turn this threat into an opportunity.

# START WITH ONE THING

The processes that I shared in this book took us years to build. You can get there faster, but you can only do one thing at a time.

I read a lot of business books. A book is worth my time if I can get one good idea from it and apply it to my business. The key word there is *apply*. Start with one idea and use it to change something in your business. That change could be a strategy, a process, or a person.

**What is the one thing that you can start doing today that will have the biggest impact on your business?**

If you are not sure where to start, go back to chapter one and work on your mission, vision, and values. If you are already set there, skim through chapters two through ten until you find something actionable that can provide immediate value for you and your team.

Once you make that happen, you can come back for more ideas. Just start with that one thing. Write it down right now. It won't be any easier to do it tomorrow.

Keep growing.

# ABOUT CAREERPLUG

Since 2007 CareerPlug has worked to make hiring easier for thousands of growing companies. We designed our software for non-HR people so every owner, operator, and hiring manager can hire and develop the right people for their team.

You can learn more about us at www.careerplug.com

# ADDITIONAL RESOURCES

Throughout this book, we've mentioned templates, guides, and other free resources that you can utilize for your business. All of these resources are available on **www.howtohire.com.**

**Chapter 2**

Compelling Careers Page Checklist

**Chapter 3**

Talent GPA Exercise

Performance Improvement Plan Template

Ideal Candidate Profile Template

**Chapter 4**

Job Posting Builder

Value/Cost Per Hire Calculator

Grade Your Application Experience

**Chapter 6**

Lifeline Interview Guide

**Chapter 7**

Hiring Process Design Worksheet

Guide to Reference and Background Checks

Candidate Defense Template

**Chapter 8**

Onboarding Checklist

90 Day Plan Template

Growth Plan Template

# RECOMMENDED READING

*Think and Grow Rich*, Napoleon Hill

*Vivid Vision*, Cameron Herold

*The Advantage*, Patrick Lencioni

*Mindset*, Carol Dweck

*Good to Great*, Jim Collins

*Radical Candor*, Kim Scott

*The Great Game of Business*, Jack Stack

*The E-Myth Revisited*, Michael Gerber

*The Five Dysfunctions of a Team*, Patrick Lencioni

*Getting Things Done*, David Allen

*The 22 Immutable Laws of Marketing*, Al Ries & Jack Trout

*Drive*, Daniel Pink

*The Sales Acceleration Formula*, Mark Roberge

*The Culture Code*, Daniel Coyle

*The Dream Manager*, Matthew Kelly

*Superbosses*, Sydney Finkelstein

*Fierce Conversations*, Susan Scott

*Traction*, Gino Wickman

*The Daily Stoic*, Ryan Holiday

# ACKNOWLEDGMENTS

First, I would like to thank my wife, Sarah, for all of her support over the past fifteen years of my entrepreneurial journey. I could not have done it without you!

I would have nothing to write about without all of the employees who helped me build CareerPlug over the years. There are too many names to list, but please know that I am truly grateful for your contributions.

Beyond the authors listed in the Recommended Reading section, there are a few mentors that have influenced my thinking about people, culture, and life in general. Ted Oakley, Mark Willis, and Mary Kennedy Thompson: thank you for your investment in me.

Finally, there are a handful of people who made this book a reality. Natalie Morgan has been there for me as an editor, coach, and project manager from the start. Thank you for your kindness and patience through this entire process. David Colby made meaningful contributions to the manuscript and helped me keep it simple. Brandy Lee provided valuable input and helped me stay organized. Vi Chetan designed the book cover, and the CareerPlug marketing team, particularly Desiree Echevarria, Kacie Sommers, Becca Cinfio, and Lauren Torregrossa, helped us get this thing published!